It All Abides in Love

In Search of the Science of Maharajji

Jai Ram Ransom

"When you have started on the path to God, proceed,
do not stop. He will take care of you."

I

It All Abides in Love
Maharajji Neem Karoli Baba
Version 1.0

Taos Music & Art, Inc.
P. O. Box 2627
Taos, New Mexico USA 87571
taosmusicandart.com

maharajji.com

ISBN-10: 0990718220
ISBN-13: 978-0-9907182-2-2

We believe in Reincarnation.
We believe in Miracles.
We believe in Surrender.
We believe in Service.

Table of Contents

Introduction   8

Maharajji Means Love 13

    Lila - Play of the Gods   14
    The Lilas Are the Teaching   17
    Divine Renunciate   19
    Maharajji Exhibited All the Siddhis   21
    Great King   22
    Lakshmi Narayan Sharma   24
    A Worthy Role Model   26
    Maharajji Is Basically Secret 27
    Maharajji Wasn't Like Us   30
    The Photo Sees   31
    Archetype of a Fully Realized Being 32
    Maharajji is The Master   34

All Religions are the Same   37

    Simplified View   37
    God Is Not a Being   38

Surrender Is Everything   42

    It's All About You   44
    Life Is Your Own Movie   47
    What Is Samsara?   48
    There Is Only the Now   49
    Nama Rupa Sat Chit Ananda 49
    Devotion   50
    Meeting Your Guru 52
    You Have a Plan for Your Own Life 54
    You Are Never Alone 55

Consciousness 57

    Where Human Consciousness Comes From 57
    Belief One: 57

Belief Two: 59
Individual Consciousness   60
The Hologram Is All There Is   62
Consciousness Manipulates DNA   62
You Are God   64
Jivatma Is Not Subservient   66
Karma and Reincarnation (Transmigration of
Souls)   66
Karma Is Your Course of Study   68
Incarnations   69
Transmigrational Amnesia   73
Transitory Worldly Attachment   75
Each Life "Scores" a One   77
Why Do We Take Birth"?   78
Life Is Experiential   79
Opening of Consciousness   79
Did LSD Open the Door?   82
Human Mind   84
Truth   87
There Is Apparent Chaos   88

It's All Maharajji   91

Maharajji Raised the Dead   91
Maharajji Was in Two Places at Once   93
Asking Maharajji   95
Listening to Maharajji   101
You Are Playing a Role in a Theater   102
The 60s   103
To Awaken You   105
Maharajji Can Speak Through You   107
Touching of the Feet   110
A Different Form of Misdirection   113
Impossible Experiences for Devotees   114
Maharajji Is a Manifestation   120

Love Is a Force   123

Circle of Beliefs   126
Devotees - Satsang   128
Miracles of Saints   135

Seva   139

A Sort of Madness   141
Tapasya   142
Human Desires Don't Matter   144
Maharajji Forgives   146
Ram Ram   147
A New Archetype   151
The Beautiful World 153
The Gods Are Deaf   158

Playing with Time   165

Those Who See that Maharajji Creates the
Circumstances Are Graced.   167
Maharajji Chooses His Devotees   170

Practice 178

Kirtan   179
Hanuman Chalisa   183
Vinaya Chalisa   185
Puja 186
Remembering Maharajji   187

Guru - Guruism - Guruist   190

Guru of Gurus   191
Maharajji Bhaktis   193
See God in Everything   196

Maharajji's India   197

India Yatra   197
Why Was Maharajji in India? 199
Ashoka the Great   201
"I Build Beautiful Temples"   202
Maharajji Had Many Rules   204
Sacrosanct Tradition 206

Temples Are for Everyone   208
Feed Everyone   210
Bhandara   211
Vrindavan Ashram   214
Kainchi Ashram   217
Bhumiadar Ashram   217
Akbarpur Janambhumi Temple   218
Other Ashrams   218
Taos - Beautiful People Everywhere   219

Dancing in the Two   223

The Seen and Unseen   225
Maharajji Speaks Internally   228
Now You Run It for Me   230
Looking for Maharajji   231
Who Makes the Rules?   234
Maharajji Seen in USA   236
Maharajji in Amarkantak   238
I'd Run Right After Him   239
Maharajji Knows Everything 245
There Is No More Randomness   248
Meek Shall Inherit the Earth 251
For the Next Generations   252

Pushpanjali to Maharajji   255

About This Book   260

Dedications   262

Endnotes266

Introduction

It's probably not necessary for every single story of Maharajji's Lilas to be retold perfectly and precisely every time. That is one important reason that books of the stories have been printed and distributed, and that the website of Maharajji was developed. These are the stories that are "etched in stone" because they are important. But Maharajji is not about history. These aren't history lessons, at all. This isn't a story of a man who was born in India, lived a life and then died. That is apparently not even remotely what happened, and indeed what is happening.

Maharajji's Lilas have been going on for a very long time. It is only now that these ongoing Lilas are being revealed on a vastly broader scale than ever before. The truth is the most important thing of all about Maharajji is now we know that Maharajji exists. You might think that "exists" should be said in the past tense. That would be wrong. The stories of these Lilas are not simply historical events. They are examples of what is a newly realized phenomenon that has finally been discovered.

Those who delve deeply into the stories of these Lilas come to realize that it is impossible for the energy of a being such as Maharajji to cease His activities among us. Maharajji is the manifest force behind all that is good in the world. They will just go on and on.

This is because these Lilas are an energy that is beginning to be realized by the humans on Earth.

Maharajji didn't do these things. No human can do what is attributed to Maharajji. Understanding that a being, a manifestation of a being, such as Maharajji on Earth is the next step in realizing the full human potential to break away from the greedy, gluttonous, envious, fearful, repressive, and war-like tendencies of the non-realized humans associating primarily with their overly-mental animal minds.

Maharajji is an example of a being that walks within the chaos of the world, yet One who sits apart from and above our old understanding of how everyone must live in the world. Maharajji represents a new reality in the world. How is it possible that Maharajji did what He did in the world? How is it even remotely possible for Him to do these Lilas? It is so easy for limited minds to not believe any of it. That's perfectly okay, because the human race is evolving.

The kids of the new millennium are evolved beyond the previous generations. It is actually a new world and the consciousness of so many of the young ones is much more spiritually conscious. They are way more open to understanding that you just call Maharajji, just focus on Maharajji within you and look for the Lilas of Maharajji to appear on the outside. Not all people are capable of that. But if you are one of those few that is capable of realizing who Maharajji is and what He represents, then this is because you have somehow become ready through your longing to be close to the true God and to live with God's benign, peaceful love, rather than to wander lost in a wilderness of manipulation, lacking in love, understanding, compassion, kindness and empathy.

Just because God manifested Himself to us in such a strange, humble, unattached, yet powerful being as Maharajji Neem Karoli Baba, for what seems to be a limited time, does not by any means signify that God's recent appearance on Earth is limited. God is still here. There is no separation. God is not floating "up there" somewhere. He is right in the midst of us. Now we know more about God and the play of the Real God (Supreme Consciousness) is beginning to be noticed in the world more and more.

This book about Maharajji that I am writing in this pleasant house an hour north of Chiang Mai Thailand is not being written for mass consumption. It is not being written to appear on the bestseller list. I am writing this because, after 30 years of research and study of Neem Karoli Baba Maharajji, I know some things. I am now dredging up these bits of information about Maharajji and the scene around Maharajji from within me and writing them down. Maybe this could be called cathartic (providing psychological relief) for me, but there is more to it. There is always much more to it with Maharajji. I have found that I am full of this material and being older now, it is time to write it down for the *satsang*.

Please do not mistake the writings in this volume to be proselytizing, marketing or promotion of Maharajji. As said, Maharajji does not require this. This volume could best be describes as "sharing." Maharajji is essentially "secret." Maharajji selects only those who are ready to become His devotees. It is not possible to convince people of the truth of Maharajji's existence. It is only the action of Maharajji with individuals that is of importance. You will not likely be drawn to reading what is contained herein about Maharajji unless Maharajji has previously selected you and in some way drawn or directed you to read this.

Sometimes, in the sort-of bhakti state that doing this writing *seva* creates in me, my writing can wander. You might notice that. I would urge you to find the core thread of this discussion and use the endnotes to learn more about the topic. I am not a master writer, but I have written this for you because Maharajji has caused me to have learned too much, seen too much, and experienced too much, after being pulled into service for Maharajji, to remain silent. Maharajji...!!! How is it possible? Can you believe it? Well, in my case firstly - I don't know how it is possible. Secondly, Yes. I can believe it.

This is about finding the most precious lotus flower jewel amazing person of light and love. A little man in a little world who was actually bigger than all of the universe, if one believes the reports. Maharajji's images and stories ARE The Story, and they are worthy of the deepest contemplation. All of us have so much that we can learn from Maharajji about how to be a force for good in the world. Indeed, perhaps you can learn to do your own miracles. Maharajji manipulated this game in such perfect ways, and yet He always remains hidden, as even now.

This writing is not "making a case" to prove anything about Maharajji to anyone. Rather this writing is for those who are experiencing the Lila of Maharajji or are just generally attracted to Maharajji because He has caught their attention in some way. The purpose of this book is to give you some information that may be helpful about the Lilas of Maharajji that continue to this day. Maharajji will prove the words herein or He will not. It is in His hands.

Be Love.

Maharajji Means Love

If you even partially believe the stories of Neem Karoli Baba, you will come to realize that Maharajji is as alive now as He ever was. The being described in the stories of Maharajji is not capable of dying. He is always here on Earth, in one body or another. Maharajji is "spirit." It was told to me some years ago, that Maharajji has been on Earth over 2,000 years. He simply "leaves His body" when it gets old, then gets a new one.

Maharajji once said, "The body has to finish." Usha Bahadur narrated that shortly before Maharajji left His body, He said to Usha, "Soon I will get a new body. This body has become very old." Usha laughed. She said that it never occurred to her that Maharajji would actually leave the body.

Just because you cannot "see" Maharajji does not mean He is not there. For those to whom Maharajji is the Guru, He is always felt. Once He has gotten hold of you He is always there with you. If at any time you do not feel Him, then simply get quiet, calm your mind, cease activities, pull yourself out of the illusion of your day and open to feeling Him there with you, and you will come to realize again that He is there.

Maharajji was not simply a person. Maharajji is "a Force," an Immortal Force of Love and Good. Maharajji is the greatest enigma of human kind. It seems He manifests in different bodies or indeed the same body in various eras. He was also caught many times being in several places at the same time. I once stood on the second floor in the back of Maharajji's Vrindavan Ashram[1] with Kabir Das and Shivaya Baba. They laughed and said, "It is so strange that they built a *mahasamadhi* temple, on the spot where Maharajji's last known body was cremated, when there is ample proof that Maharajji had several bodies."

राम राम राम राम राम राम राम राम राम राम राम राम

Lila - Play of the Gods

In Hindi, *Lila* means "the play of the Gods." One who has entered the Lila of Maharajji begins to realize that something else is going on..., that there is now some other force at work in their lives. That there is now a guardian angel who is there to experience their lives with them and indeed to create their life's experience for them. In the surrender to this Lila of Maharajji's Love one finds the practice of the living of daily life different. When one realizes Maharajji, there is no longer the thoughts that You are just an animal who is playing out a limited drama of self indulgence, but that you are also an immortal being playing an ongoing multi-life play of existence along with many other beings who have also realized (or not realized) this.

Maharajji knows you. Maharajji knows all about you. Maharajji has a plan for you. Maharajji actually IS you. How can this be? Maharajji said, "It is better to see God in everything than to try to figure it all out." It has been said that the first step on the "Spiritual Path" is to realize who the real You is. Who am I? Who am I, Really? Well you are more than your mind "thinks" you are.

Maharajji is the teacher who never taught by traditional means. Maharajji would hit you in the head, or pull your beard, or yank your hair, or say strange things about you, or fill you with food and put you to sleep. Maharajji taught through His Lila. When there is something happening, it is Maharajji's Lila. When there is nothing happening, it is Maharajji's Lila. You are feeling well, it is Maharajji's Lila. You are feeling sick, it is Maharajji's Lila. When you are rich or when you are poor, it is Maharajji's Lila.

There are thousands of stories of the Lilas of Maharajji. For one who digests all of these stories, a realization within you begins to develop that life is not exactly how you thought it was. That's why it is a bit scary, at first. You realize that you seem to have prematurely closed accounts with reality..., with what reality is. But for all this talk of Guru, and the fact that Maharajji is known as "The Guru of Gurus," it must be said that Maharajji isn't really a Guru. Maharajji is the Avatar[2] of this Age. Maharajji is a manifestation of God in human form..., a fully realized divine manifestation of God. Again, how can this be? No one knows.

The Lila of Maharajji as the Avatar of this age is quite different than the manifestation of the other Avatars of Lord Vishnu such as Lord Krishna, Lord Ram, and Lord Buddha. Maharajji is the manifestation of God as a complete renunciate who had all the powers of all the Gods. Within Maharajji was *Atma* (*Atman*)(meaning all of us and everything) rather than *Jivatma* (*Jivatman*) (an individual soul entity). Maharajji is not simply the *Avatar* of Vishnu such as Ram, Krishna and Buddha. Maharajji is the appearance of a Super Avatar of Vishnu, Shiva, Brahma, as well as Hanumanji all in one.

Maharajji does His Lilas to call attention to; to attract the devotee to the path to Maharajji, to direct them to seek more, to cause them to seek answers to the questions brought about by these Lilas. Lilas can be very small or quite large. Lilas can manifest as short-term events, or the Lila can play out over many years. Long-term Lilas are not easy to catch because of the passage of such a long time. These Lilas surely "unfold," rather than "strike."

Maybe Maharajji is here for "fun." Maybe it's fun taking care of His devotees as they live out physical incarnations. There are so many stories told by devotees about how much fun it was hanging out with

Maharajji, and how Maharajji would make them laugh so much. Devotees utterly loved being with Maharajji. Since Lila means "play of the Gods," performing Lilas must be fun.

राम राम राम राम राम राम राम राम राम राम राम राम

The Lilas Are the Teaching

Maharajji did so many of these Lilas as teachings, as examples that would go into the books of stories about Him. Maharajji never really gave teachings, as such. He never really sat down and gave lessons. His teachings were examples that people would learn from because of having experienced them. It has been said that Maharajji did not give formal teachings because no one could truly hear him, because no one truly understood.

Someone asked Maharajji why he didn't give teachings (I assume, he was asking why Maharajji didn't give "lectures"). Maharajji asked various people around His tucket what they were going to do the next day. They gave answers that described their usual day of mundane activities of work, etc.. Maharajji then pointed out that each person already had a program of what they would do with their lives planned out and nothing He could say would change that. Maharajji is certainly working in His own way rather than the obvious method of giving lessons to devotees. Nevertheless, Maharajji could and did indeed change the destinies of His devotees. It is His play to refute

His ability to teach anything. Maharajji expressed many teachings directly to devotees. Maharajji was and is teaching His devotees even now long after His last known body was cremated in Vrindavan so many years ago.

The answers are given in the thousands of individual stories of Maharajji's Lila. They are the teachings – by example. Each story of Maharajji's Lilas is worthy of contemplation in much the same way as a *Zen Koan*[3]. Each story has a message for His devotee. Maharajji taught in this way. There is much to learn from these stories and many are worthy of your deep contemplation and should be long remembered and often remembered. Devotees of Maharajji will find it very helpful to frequently use bits of the teachings in these stories as signposts and gentle reminders as they tread along the spiritual path of their lives. Each quotation of Maharajji is certainly worthy of the same contemplation.

Of course Maharajji used these sorts of Lilas as a teaching tool. Maharajji was riding in the back seat of the car. Gurudat Sharma was riding beside Him. There was a driver in the front and also another man. Sharmaji is a very proper Brahman. He always does his practice in silence. However, this time he suddenly began to sing "Sri Ram Jai Ram Jai Jai Ram" very loudly with his voice. Maharajji immediately yelled at him saying, "Do your practice in silence." Gurudat claimed that Maharajji had caused him to sing like that so that He could give instruction to the passenger in the front of the car. Thus Maharajji was able to instruct this man through a little drama.

The core of the perception of Maharajji is the Lilas. The Lilas are Maharajji's use of the powers of the unseen physical and non-physical to manifest on the physical. Everything about Maharajji is Lila. If you are conscious of having entered the Lila of Maharajji, you know exactly what is meant by this.

राम राम राम राम राम राम राम राम राम राम राम राम

Divine Renunciate

Maharajji in the form of Neem Karoli Baba could be described as a hobo or a tramp. He certainly was a divine renunciate. Maharajji is a *sadhu*. Maharajji had nothing and Maharajji had everything. Maharajji lived as a person who was very poor but Maharajji was very rich in the sense that whatever Maharajji summoned simply appeared as necessary. Maharajji was quoted as saying, "All the money in the world is mine, even the money in America."

The devotees of Maharajji in India believe that Maharajji is the direct manifestation of the Hindu God Hanuman. There is a story of Maharajji wherein He appears to Dada as Hanuman in such a way that He seems to have blown Dada's mind out for some time. In one case Maharajji was speaking about Hanuman and referred to Hanuman saying the "I" pronoun in place of Hanuman. There is a story where Maharajji's palms and soles of His feet turned red like Hanuman. Also cited are stories of how much Maharajji loved to climb in the trees, and there is in fact a tree remaining in Akbarpur[4] that the villagers say Maharajji frequently climbed.

Mukunda wrote in Prem Avatar, "Shri Baba Neem Karoli Maharaj was the manifestation of God or the incarnation himself. He was the paramGuru, he was the absolute God or complete being, he was the treasury of grace, of kindness, of forgiveness, and he was the very fountain of blissful love for God. He was also the giver of that blissful love for God to others."[5]

राम राम राम राम राम राम राम राम राम राम राम राम

Maharajji was known as the "Miracle Baba." Many stories tell of a great number of miracles attributed to Maharajji. Some of these miracles are absolutely blatant, and some are absolutely subtle. Maharajji raised the dead. Maharajji turned water into milk and into petrol. Maharajji appeared in two or more places at the same time. Maharajji invisibly caught children who fell out of tall buildings. Maharajji became invisible and made devotees with Him invisible, too. Maharajji made food appear where there was no food. Maharajji cured illnesses and caused others to cure illnesses. Maharajji's clothes suddenly changed as He walked with devotees. Maharajji knew all about everyone, past, present, future. Maharajji could open someone's heart and throw them into deep love with a glance.

But Maharajji was not doing any miracles. Maharajji was doing Science. It is a science that the human race does not know, has not discovered. Maharajji's science can be learned by anyone because we are the same being as Maharajji deep deep within our collective Atman. We have the example set for us by Maharajji to know that such work is possible and to realize the extent of the possibilities of these miracles, of this science that works in unseen ways.

राम राम राम राम राम राम राम राम राम राम राम राम

Maharajji Exhibited All the Siddhis

"Siddhis (सिद्धि) are spiritual, magical, supranormal, paranormal, or supernatural powers acquired through sadhana (spiritual practices), such as meditation and yoga. People who have attained this state are formally known as siddhas. In Hinduism eight siddhis (Ashta Siddhi) are known: Aṇimā: reducing one's body even to the size of an atom, Mahima: expanding one's body to an infinitely large size, Garima: becoming infinitely heavy, Laghima: becoming almost weightless, Prāpti: having unrestricted access to all places, Prākāmya: realizing whatever one desires, Iṣṭva: possessing absolute lordship, and Vaśtva: the power to subjugate all."[6]

I think many of the devotees of Maharajji's satsang have developed secret siddhis. They will never admit to that, ever, for then these powers are lost. Nevertheless, the siddhis are there. Maharajji grants these to us in large and small ways. Sometimes they are temporary. Some are earned. Some are a total "gift." I have observed through the years that among these siddhis is an extra level of telepathy between His devotees.

राम राम राम राम राम राम राम राम राम राम राम राम

Great King

In India, the term Maharajji is very broad. It essentially means "Great King." It is often applied to many sorts of people. However, here we are speaking of the Maharajji who manifested as the one called Neem Karoli Baba, Neem Karoli Wali Baba, Neeb Karori Baba, Lakshman Das Baba, Talaya Walla Baba (the baba of the lake), Handi Walla Baba (baba with the broken piece of clay pot), and several other names in India. Maharajji showed each and every attribute of God above and beyond all of the other true Babas. Yet there are so many false prophets, so many, many false Maharajjis, false babas, mental babas who are driven by greed and power and lust and even anger. This has always been the problem with the human race.

Maharajji redefines the many manifestations of God from a human perspective. In a sense Maharajji is a new God. Maharajji is "The Maharajji of Maharajjis."

राम राम राम राम राम राम राम राम राम राम राम राम

Lakshmi Narayan Sharma

Neem Karoli Baba seems to have been born Lakshmi Narayan Sharma in Akbarpur. Yet there are so many mysteries about the timelines of His life that we cannot be certain of what transpired. An important aspect is the one that Maharajji apparently identified as his first "teacher," Mataji Ram Bai, a lady saint in Bavania (Vavania) Gujarat in western India. When He was quite young, Maharajji lived at the *ashram* of Ram Bai. Maharajji apparently acknowledged this. Yet Ram Bai, according to Western researcher Raj Agni, left her body in about 1897, before Lakshmi Narayan Sharma was born. How is that possible? There are other indications Maharajji gave that the timeline associated with Lakshmi Narayan Sharma is not necessarily His timeline. And how is it possible that Maharajji could be in several places at one time? I've been told that Maharajji appears to have been a "time traveler." That, in and of itself, implies that He is a supernatural entity. Does that explain the anomaly with Ram Bai?

Maharajji left two names by which He is best known worldwide. These names are "Baba Neeb Karori" and "Neem Karoli Baba." In India, there are often many ways of pronouncing the same word(s). The village of Neeb Karori (sometimes spelled "Nibkarori"), where Maharajji resided for some time in the 1930s is the principal source of the name. In essence, the meaning is "the baba from Neeb Karori." However, the village name is alternately pronounced

"Neeb Karori" or "Neem Karoli" in common daily speech. So, you can see, it's complicated. Ram Dass and the Western satsang picked up on the "Neem Karoli Baba" version and that name was brought to the West, and it was spread globally. More properly, Maharajji's name would be pronounced (and written) as "Baba Neeb Karori." However, there is also the case that at the time Maharajji was called Lakshman Das when He lived in Neeb Karori village. Maharajji's birth name is Lakshmi Narayan Sharma. In this manner, Maharajji has encompassed a greater area of names. These create more ways for His devotees to find Him. The Lila of Maharajji's names seems to matter little to the true devotee of Maharajji. When any and all of Maharajji's names are spoken these devotees are becoming happy and at peace.[7]

राम राम राम राम राम राम राम राम राम राम राम राम

Was Neem Karoli Baba a "walk-in"? Was he someone who was just a normal person and in the course of His *sadhana*[8] became inhabited by a greater entity that was infinite, fully conscious and supernatural? No. Maharajji is far greater than that.

Maharajji is the most amazing being I have ever even heard of. Every movie star, every billionaire industrialist, every superb creative artist, every president, every prime minister, every king, every queen, all pale by comparison. They are all rather caught in the illusion of who they think they are and who others think they are. Yet it is not who they are - it is who they are being, the role they are playing in this life. This is not to take away from the feats of people who achieve greatness in the world. You know who. Utterly amazing, totally charmed, lives have played out before us in the media, all in just the past 100 years, as well as the preceding thousands of years of history. Many have connected with their Jivatmas and manifest that connection in the world. Yet, Maharajji played no role. There was no one home there. He just wasn't there to be an ego.

राम राम राम राम राम राम राम राम राम राम राम राम

A Worthy Role Model

Maharajji healed the sick, calmed the angry, cured the insane, comforted the persons in need, turned water into milk, made food appear from nowhere, raised the dead, helped to advance His devotee's spiritual evolution, and much more. Is He not a worthy role model?

It is easy to look at Maharajji as being something outside of us, yet every one of His devotees, and indeed all people, can potentially do these things. Maharajji is not a distant being. Maharajji is a close being. Maharajji is not some sort of William the Conqueror high upon a throne ready to wreak his vengeance upon you for no reason, or even for a very good reason.

You cannot hurt Maharajji. Nothing can be done to hurt Maharajji. No words or deeds can affect Maharajji. Maharajji doesn't require "public relations" in order to exist, nor can Maharajji be "marketed." Maharajji works from the inside outwardly, yet He also works on the "outside," in the world, to show the way and guide devotees.

Maharajji said, "It is not necessary to meet your Guru on the physical plane. The Guru is not external."

राम राम राम राम राम राम राम राम राम राम राम राम

Maharajji Is Basically Secret

Maharajji is basically secret. Maharajji is not for all the masses. This may come about much later. Maharajji is the head of a family. The family is called the satsang. There is no way to join the satsang. Only Maharajji invites.

Maharajji is so subtle, as well as secret. Even Steve Jobs said, "...Thomas Edison did a lot more to improve the world than Karl Marx and Neem Karoli Baba put together. " That is "so Maharajji" to make Steve Jobs say that. Of course, Maharajji would hide and never allow His part to be revealed. It's so typical. There was a simple doctor in India to whom Maharajji would send sick people. The doctor was asked about this after some years and he said that he never gave the sick people anything more than the usual medicines, yet even the people with serious diseases were cured. He had not met Maharajji but had always wondered who the baba was who was doing this. When asked, Maharajji said that the doctor did it all because he was a great doctor. I feel that Jobs was another one of those who came to Maharajji's attention because he took LSD, and that he was of course manipulated and guided through many Lilas for the benefit of the whole human race.

राम राम राम राम राम राम राम राम राम राम राम राम

There is no organization that you can "join" to be in Maharajji's satsang. It doesn't work that way. You won't get a prescribed course of study or be given a specific path to follow. There is nothing like that. It is an ultimate self-study course. That doesn't mean that you (your mind) can just invent a belief structure around Maharajji. You can say that there are no rules. You can say there are many rules that are enforced strictly. You can say that every one of the Ten Commandments must be followed and you can say that these have no bearing on anything. The thread is Love. There is no other thread but Love. There is no other religion but Love. Do not be deluded. Maharajji has left many clues to help you decipher who he is and these will lead you on the spiritual path..., and to possibly some understanding of the science used by Maharajji.

This all could be called the "Maharajji Movement." Maybe we could call it the "Neem Karoli Baba Movement," too. But that isn't what it really is because that is way too small. It really is the Lila of Maharajji beginning in the 20th Century with the form we have come to know, in the West, as Neem Karoli Baba. Maharajji's Lilas have gone on for probably millennia. The form of Maharajji that has appeared in the age of huge population and instantaneous media communication is that of a very humble yet omnipotent man. Shivaya Baba, an American who was with Maharajji in the 70s, once said that he thought the biggest miracles of Maharajji are what have happened since He left His body. Maharajji in form went away from His devotees, but the Lilas did not. It is as if Maharajji has stepped into the next room and will return any minute.

राम राम राम राम राम राम राम राम राम राम राम राम

As our Guru, Maharajji removes the darkness and allows the light within us to shine upon every cell of our body and the others around us. The human games play out all around because we are all in human form just as Maharajji assumed a human form. Yet Maharajji is the essence of *Sat Chit Ananda*. Maharajji is unchanging and unaffected. Maharajji is always there. Maharajji is always here. Are we not trying to actually be Maharajji? However, to take the steps to begin this path requires that we drop our illusions and attachments.

राम राम राम राम राम राम राम राम राम राम राम राम

Maharajji Wasn't Like Us

Maharajji wasn't like "us." Maharajji didn't think like us. Maharajji didn't act like us. Maharajji didn't react like us. Maharajji didn't do things the way we do things. Neem Karoli Baba wasn't in the Time-Space Continuum as we are. It could be said that Maharajji wasn't/isn't a human. He appeared as a human body that we refer to as Neem Karoli Baba. He had arms, legs, eyes, and ears, like all of us. He had feet; much revered and beloved feet – lotus feet. What does this mean? How is this possible? It is almost incomprehensible. That is Maharajji. This is what makes Maharajji worthy of the deepest study and contemplation. By turning to Him with love and devotion to your understanding, a realization may begin to develop.

Dada wrote this about Maharajji, "We all know that Babaji has been a human being with human form and shape. But if we confine our attention merely to the physical, to the body, we cannot understand him. We find that even with the physique of a human being, he had the energy, he had the power, he had the love and affection that does not come to a human being. The greatest human beings of whom we read in history, no doubt they have done and achieved so many things. But what Babaji, or a saint like him, could achieve was certainly not in the capacity of the individual human being. If that is so, we must conclude that in the human body there was some force, some authority, that was not human."9

Mataji said that when one fully realizes who Maharajji is, they are completely shaken to the very depths of their being. This may appear to even be a form of insanity to others because people's minds cannot grasp what is happening and can lose their grip on reality. This is because there is nothing in human life to train one to understand or comprehend that such a being as Maharajji even exists among us on earth.

राम राम राम राम राम राम राम राम राम राम राम राम

The Photo Sees

The Hindus believe that the *murti* (sculpture) of the God sees. By extension, this also means that the photographs also see you. The Hindus do not so much go to the temple to see the sculpted manifestation of God, but rather for the deity to see them. There are so many cases where devotees of Maharajji go to the photo of Maharajji to ask for something that is then forthcoming. The devotee prays to the photo and Maharajji answers the prayer.

Maharajji gives His *darshan* through photos of Him. If you have seen a photo of Maharajji you might be drawn to finding out more about Maharajji. There is not much in the way of teaching about Maharajji. Most information about Maharajji is contained in several books of stories of Maharajji's Lila's, a web site at maharajji.com, and from others who know something worthwhile about Maharajji.

राम राम राम राम राम राम राम राम राम राम राम राम

Why is Maharajji different? Well actually the question maybe should be: Why are You different from Maharajji? The seed of consciousness is within you as with all beings on Earth. So who is/was Maharajji? Was Maharajji an alien? Was Maharajji a manifestation in the way Krishna describes himself to Arjuna in the Bhagavad Gita?[10] Was Maharajji a normal man who had grown extraordinary powers? Was Maharajji a kriya yogi? I have heard that some believe that Maharajji is the Babaji from "Autobiography of a Yogi" by Paramahansa Yogananda.

Archetype of a Fully Realized Being

Maharajji is actually what Everyone is looking for – an archetype of a fully realized being who knows everything about you in this life and other lives and who totally loves you..., an archetype of a fully realized being who is not attached, a wandering aesthetic, barefoot, sleeping outside in the open, spending His days up in the trees, having nothing, desiring nothing, attached to nothing, living only for His devotees, uncatchable, an utterly enigmatic being, meaning one whose ways simply cannot be understood.

राम राम राम राम राम राम राम राम राम राम राम राम

According to Baba C. S. Sharma, when Maharajji first left Akbarpur as a boy of ten, more than a hundred years ago, he first went to Ayodhya. There He was greeted by a group of Sadhus (renunciate holy men). The leader of the sadhus saw the boy and began yelling, "He has arrived. Hanuman has come to us. We have waited so long. Now He is here." The sadhus took Him in. Later Maharajji went west to Bavania.

At Maharajji's Vrindavan Ashram in 1996, I asked, a Canadian baba, Kabir Das, if he thought Neem Karoli Baba might be an "alien." Kabir replied, "Maharajji was the highest form of human evolution." This implies that Maharajji was a normal human that through *tapasya* austerities, renunciation, Hindu practices, and other practices we can't possibly know, achieved a fully realized state of consciousness and developed the power to do His Lilas. This also implies that more humans will be able to "develop" the powers exhibited by Maharajji as the race evolves. I am not so sure I agree with this, because after many years of studying Maharajji, I have come to believe that Maharajji is actually a manifested supernatural being.

Shivaya Baba said, "Maybe someday there will be thousands of Neem Karoli Babas wandering around America." This is a comforting thought due to Maharajji's love and benign care of us. The quantum physics aspects of Maharajji cannot be denied. Claiming supernatural powers for someone is not something usual in this world. However, people seem to believe that supernatural powers exist, or at least fantasize that they are real through movies and books.

राम राम राम राम राम राम राम राम राम राम राम राम

Maharajji is The Master

Maharajji is the guide, Maharajji is the master. At sometime on the future physical plane timeline, all are Maharajji because the Jivatma souls riding in the bodies have realized that they are not animals, that Jivatma did not arise from primordial ooze, although this is what their physical plane bodies evolved from.

Maharajji won't randomly mess around with your *karma*. Your karma is, well, your karma. Yet Maharajji seems to mitigate karma for His devotees. Perhaps it is your karma to get sick and Maharajji will help by making your illness less severe. Maybe you are never destined to wed and have children but He will bring you into a happy association with many young people. However, Maharajji said, "I am capable of changing destiny. There is no power in the world that can go against what I have said. I can lower the exalted and raise the humble." This is a very profound statement, and worthy of the deepest contemplation.

Maharajji is not by any means a "New Age" phenomenon. It's almost silly to think that. Maharajji is not a hokus pokus hustle. Maharajji is as real as real can be. He always has been utterly real and always will be utterly real. He is you, He is me, He is us.

In the Prologue of his book, "I and My Father are One," Rabboo Joshi mentions, "The need of the hour is a universal Guru, who would be a Grand Master, both, in Science and Spirituality. This Guru, will re-align the Yin and Yang of ailing humanity. All religions have to seek a common plot form and give space to science in their life to better their suffering lot. This Guru need not be in a body. It could be a set of precepts and principles universally applicable. This Guru, when accepted by one and all, will ultimately give individual space to every one to practice spirituality. Once you are truly spiritual you cannot hurt even a fly. All the masters of the past never founded a religion, they only taught spirituality. Be it Jesus Christ, Prophet Mohammed, Buddha, Mahavir, Shankara Charya, Zoroaster, the followers subsequently founded the religion. All hatred, violence, assertiveness, aggression are the byproducts of religion, which the original masters never taught their disciples."[11]

Maharajji transcends everything ever created or invented on the physical plane. He has been guiding us for more than two thousand years and He will not stop. He cannot be diminished or removed because He is within all. There is no group to join. There is no organization. There are precious few guides you can trust. Awaken to the real truth. Be enlightened by the light of love. Practice peace and the greater love. Always seek to operate using a greater understanding. Operate under the eternal universal Golden Rule, as taught by Jesus "Do to others as you would have them do to you."

राम राम राम राम राम राम राम राम राम राम राम राम

All Religions are the Same

Maharajji said, "All religions are the same. They all lead to God. God is everybody... the same blood flows through us all, the arms, the legs, the heart, all are the same. See no difference. See all the same."

Simplified View

There are really only three "religions": Hinduism, Buddhism, and the triad of The Tribe of Abraham – Judaism, Christianity, and Muslim. But Hinduism and Buddhism are not actually religions. They are Dharmas. The simplest way to describe *Dharma* is to say that it is a practice. It is about how you do your life on a daily basis.

Technically, everything is Hindu. Hinduism encompasses all forms of God and worship of God. Hinduism does not fit into Christianity, Mohammadism, Judaism, Buddhism, Zen, and others. However, all these and everything else fit quite nicely into Hindu belief. And in fact Buddhism, Jainism, and Sikhism are outgrowths of Hinduism. Buddha was raised in a Hindu society and is recognized by Hindus as the ninth Avatar of Lord Vishnu. One can almost hear the Hindu scholars saying, "Oh, yes yes, here is another form of God. Here is another belief system. Here is another practice." How could there be a problem? There are so many forms of God. Praise God!

Praise Atma, the God consciousness within all of us. Thou art God.

Gurudat Sharma described Dharma to me thusly, "Dharma incorporates all good things into itself. It protects you only if you protect it. Not religious - Dharma is more than that. Dharma incorporates all of the good things an individual must do for himself and others. To do good for others is the best of dharma. To inflict (pain or injury) on others is most heinous act against dharma. *Ahar** (food), *Nitra** (sleep), *Bhaya** (fear), *Methun** (Sex). These are all common in human beings and beasts. Only dharma separates human beings from animals." [*indicates Sanskrit]

Religion is about organization, an organization of beliefs. It has been said that followers of all of these religions bow at Maharajji's feet because He is a manifestation of God (Supreme Consciousness) appearing on Earth in the form of pure benign unattached Love.

राम राम राम राम राम राम राम राम राम राम राम राम

God Is Not a Being

God is not a "being." God has no gender. God has no personality. God is consciousness – pure fully realized consciousness. Consciousness created the entire physical universe and the rules that govern the creation of the physical universe. Consciousness created many other universes that do not use the same rules as the physical universe. Maharajji manifested the consciousness of God. In the western world, many people "do not believe in God." But really that is to say they do not believe in a God as has been previously described throughout history, which is a God who is "A Being," a God who lives "out there" or "up there." Of course this would happen because it is not the truth that God is a being. The essence of God consciousness is within each and every being. We all "know" this if we search inside.

There is much struggle over many centuries about the "One God." The Abrahamic religions differ from Hinduism and Buddhism in proclaiming one God. The Muslim religion is monotheistic and says the only God is Allah. Because of the concept of Father, Son and Holy Ghost, Christianity is arguably a religion of three gods. Judaism is known as a monotheistic religion, yet there are indications it is not.

As Biblical Scholar Bart D. Ehrman points out, "There are numerous other examples both in the Bible and in other Jewish texts in which angels are described as God and, just as important, in which angels are described as humans. One of the most interesting is Psalm 82. In this beautiful plea that justice be done for those who are weak and needy, we are told, in v. 1, that 'God has taken his place in the divine council; in the midst of the gods he holds judgment.' In the Job passage the divine beings making up God's council are called 'sons of God.' Here in Psalm 82 they are called 'children of the Most High.' But more than that, they are called 'Elohim' (82:6)—the Hebrew word for 'God' (it is a plural word; when not referring to God, it is usually translated as 'gods'). These angelic beings are 'gods.'"[12]

It can be said that Hindus worship 3,300,000 gods and goddesses (some say 33 million). However, these gods are "aspects" of the one God. Perhaps the One God concept in Hinduism can be best understood by the name *"Bhagavan"* (and possibly *"Prabhu"*). Bhagavan is mentioned in virtually every *puja* and *aarti*[13], yet there are no specific temples for the worship of Bhagavan and there are no specific pujas to Bhagavan as there are for the other Gods. It seems to be that to the Hindus, Bhagwan can be seen in some references as an amorphous personalized God-being such as Jehovah or Allah. Bhagavan is in many ways analogous to the general Christian conception of God. While the Buddhists do not fundamentally worship any god, I believe it can be said that they are way into consciousness. So, in that Supreme Consciousness is God Consciousness, then they are indeed "into" God.

राम राम राम राम राम राम राम राम राम राम राम राम

People of all faiths can relate to Maharajji. For the Hindus, He is the ultimate swamiji, the Guru of Gurus,

Bhagwan. For the Muslims, He is a revered *fakir* and pure soul. For the Jews, He is a master Prophet and beloved grandfather. For the Christians, He is the ultimate devotee and lover of the Christian god, Jesus. For the Buddhists, He is the essence of Buddha's teachings. For the atheist (non-believer), He transcends all stereotypes of spirituality.

राम राम राम राम राम राम राम राम राम राम राम राम

Surrender Is Everything

Amidst all this, Maharajji is/was working on people in a different way. The Lilas of Maharajji are so important to the process. The Lilas of Maharajji shake the foundations of the "reality" of the devotee to the point that what they thought was real would be called into question in their minds. Surrendering to a new reality becomes all there is. In this surrender lies the salvation of so many new life experiences. Shaking the foundations of what had been thought to be reality is the first step to freedom and some understanding. Most long-time devotees of Maharajji in this life realize that they have been with Maharajji, in service to and with Maharajji, for many, many lifetimes. Evolutionarily, it is about the freeing and tuning of the entire human race to a much higher vibration.

Maharajji's satsang have surrendered their lives to Maharajji. Maharajji called these devotees and pulled them into His Lila. At some point, they realized that this had happened and at some point they surrendered to Him. Maharajji then controlled their lives. It is as simple as that. And what happened then? Nothing fundamentally different, perhaps, but more often a manifest change occurred in often profound ways. They continued to watch the "movie" of their own lives. Yet now there was an inner knowing, an inner grasp of a different reality (a different consciousness, if you will). Now, the person knew that "it is all Maharajji" and could see Maharajji's Lila in everything.

Many of these devotees became rather fearless in their lives. It became difficult to be depressed, because all was in the control of Maharajji. The bleakest, scariest things could be faced because it was yet another Lila of Maharajji. And they often experienced the most remarkable outcomes to situations. Their lives are no longer operating along the lines of their human brains all the way down to their reptile brains at the core of their minds. They now are operating in a different way. Most devotees that I know operate as though Maharajji were just in the next room – that Maharajji is attending to everything – including the weather. How is that possible? I don't know. I just know that the devotees of satsang operate their lives in this way. They just let Maharajji move them.

There are many who are unconscious of this also. Maharajji is playing a part in the lives of many people who simply don't recognize any control by Maharajji at all. This can be family and friends. Yet Maharajji's grace, Maharajji's blessing, is there in their lives on a daily basis whether they know it or not. This is, quite naturally, the case with close family and friends of Maharajji's satsang. How could they not be affected? Grace is grace. The grace rubs off on those with whom you interact. If your friend is a devotee of Maharajji, Maharajji affects you in a very positive albeit unseen way. It may take 20 years for you to realize this or you may never realize it in this life. It matters little.

To hear, or better still, to speak the name Neem Karoli Baba, or any of the variations of that name, one must be ready. And it goes beyond that.

Maharajji said, "Go on worshipping God in thought, word, and action. Then you will be able to perform *Nishkama Karma* (deeds performed without any attachment or desire). The ability of Nishkama Karma[14] can be achieved only by His grace and cannot be acquired by any other means. None can claim a right to His grace. It is up to Him to give it, refuse it, or to take it away."[15]

We are all born with some physical powers to help us through. Maybe you have extra endurance energy or exceptional eyesight or great strength or have a photographic memory or even telepathy. Maharajji seems to enhance those innate powers and indeed gives new powers that devotees previously did not know existed.

राम राम राम राम राम राम राम राम राम राम राम राम

It's All About You

Everything about Maharajji is to get you in touch with you, to show you who you really are, to bring you into being your greater self; your greater You. That greater You is fundamentally Maharajji. Maharajji would not have even appeared in form if not for the devotees, for His children. He was not here for anything but us – particularly You. It may have appeared that he was here "for Himself" because we can apparently trace Him in time, like a normal person, but that is not the case.

Maharajji (Atma) and You (Jivatma) are doing what you are doing together in a way only known to you. Either you are spiritually evolving or you are not. Some can fudge the results to make them look good to receive favor from other humans but it will be limited. You can only surrender to Maharajji and let the rest of it play out. Surrender is everything. But it must be said that all of it is under the complete control of Maharajji.

Maharajji looks within you and sees who you really are. You do not go to Him, now. He comes to you. Yes, He may call you to His ashram or temple to "be with Him." If that is the case, you should be very open to hearing Him. Everything will be a message. The whole Lila that takes place there is the message, so observe everything. There will be moments that will "ring a bell" within your thinking. Be sensitive to those. Maharajji helps you achieve a balance between the inner and outer with these moments.

As Mukundaji so beautifully describes, "As soon as he will hear the call of a person in trouble wherever he may be then either he himself or through any other means of either a moving mean or a non-moving mean. Either he will go there himself or he will prompt others to do it. He will rescue that particular person in trouble. And, such Lilas would take place continuously in an eternal flow without any impediment with the same speed. And, they are taking place even today. And, that was the reason that he could never stay at one place. His body and his divine limbs were always moving even while we were thinking he was in samadhi or he was in deep sleep he would be present somewhere else performing his Lilas. There is no number of the [lilas and kathas][16], the tales of Babaji Maharaj, there is no limit to such things."[17]

All of us think about ourselves most of the time. Oh yes, we may be serving others in some ways, but generally we are thinking about ourselves – about body functioning like peeing or pooping, eating, being hot or cold, whether we are happy or sad, energized or fatigued. Maharajji was here for His devotees only. Maharajji said, "Dada, you should not be angry. This is the world, this is *samsara* [illusion]. Nobody comes to me for my own sake; everybody comes for their own problems."

राम राम राम राम राम राम राम राम राम राम राम राम

Life Is Your Own Movie

Life is Your Own "movie." The experience of your life. Witness the unfolding linear quality of your own life and the lives of others. Who is living that life? Is there something within you that is "the experiencer" of that life? Is that experiencer simply using your body as a vehicle in which to do the experiencing? The Hindus call the experiencer the Atman or Atma. This is from *Vedanta*[18], and particularly *Advaita Vedanta*. When you say "I" and I say "I" it is the same I.

There is also the Jivatma which is the smaller "I" that is your own experiencer within You. Your Jivatma is reborn in various bodies and carries your karma. The Jivatma transmigrates and is what the Christians call the "Soul." The Jivatma reincarnates, that is to say that this is the essence that migrates from body to body.

There is no such thing as "past lives." Time and space fundamentally do not exist. They are created by consciousness as "the movie." In the science of Maharajji, consciousness is a means to appear in multiply places at the same time, to time travel and can indeed restore life to the dead body.

The path of your life is what you were set upon with no deviation, that the "movie" of your life is there to watch and your consciousness should just pull back from the drama of it enough that you can watch your life (and many other lives) unfold before you while you reside in a place of utter love as you observe the goings on. It is much like surfing in that, once begun, the wave will take you for the ride. You, of course, take action – play out all the actions needed in your life knowing full well it is what you are destined to do.

राम राम राम राम राम राम राम राम राम राम राम राम

What Is Samsara?

This is indeed worthy of your deep contemplation and study. I came to an understanding that *Samsara* is the world, including all the *Maya* (illusion) of everything from the standpoint of our being within the physical plane through many births and deaths of bodies having our Jivatma soul consciousness. It is on one side of the thinnest of veils and represents the world of The Two. *Nirvana* is on the other side of the veil. Nirvana is defined as the state of "the imperturbable stillness of mind after the fires of desire, aversion, and delusion have been finally extinguished" (Buddhist) and "the union with the divine ground of existence Brahman (Supreme Being) and the experience of blissful ego-lessness." (Hindu).[19]

This Buddhist definition implies that Nirvana is based on a release from the physical plane mind. This is what Nirvana can be but it is not what Nirvana IS. Nirvana among Hindus is closer, describing The One or Oneness of Atma as Supreme Consciousness (Brahman noted as Supreme Being). To say we are all in

Samsara means that the physical plane, as created by consciousness, is just chugging along and we are just transmigrating in and out of Samsara based on our karmas in what seems to be an eternal process. That process, however, will end. There is an implication of *Maya* (illusion) in Samsara, because the physical plane is a hologram and the hologram is the illusion.

राम राम राम राम राम राम राम राम राम राम राम राम

There Is Only the Now

Time should be mentioned here. As implied in the title of the book "Be Here Now" there is only The Now. Past and present are illusion. I assume that, if you are reading this book, you have already deeply experienced this. It is utterly impossible to hold even one second (or nanosecond) of time. Future and Past are only abstract reference points to be used by our languages but they are not real and have never been real within the hologram of Samsara, the physical plane. They are as real and as tangible as "Now," which is of course only fleetingly real or tangible.

राम राम राम राम राम राम राम राम राम राम राम राम

Nama Rupa Sat Chit Ananda

There are only five things in the world. Two are constantly changing and three never change. The two that are ever changing are Name (*nama*) and Form (*rupa*). The three that never change are Essential

Existence (*sat*), Essential Consciousness (*chit*) and Bliss, which is really beyond bliss (*Ananda*).[20]

What are we using the vehicle (this body) for? Why are we riding in these bodies? This is where Maharajji said, "It is better to see God in everything than to try to figure it all out." Who can possibly know the why? Maharajji knows. And Maharajji plays with that, causing these Lilas. However, we are probably just riding in these bodies to experience the physical plane in a "self-aware state" of consciousness.

राम राम राम राम राम राम राम राम राम राम राम राम

Devotion

Dada and Didi, husband and wife devotees of Maharajji were utterly devoted to Maharajji in the deepest love. After Maharajji left His body, Dada spent several hours every morning creating a flower puja on Maharajji's tucket. Every afternoon Didi spent several hours making a very faithful watercolor painting of each of these flower pujas. This took place for around 14 years until Dada left his body. This amounts to a bit over 5,000 watercolor paintings created by this husband and wife team who brimmed over in love and service to Maharajji. Each painting is an expression of absolute love in tangible form and utter devotion.

राम राम राम राम राम राम राम राम राम राम राम राम

Maharajji left His Neem Karoli Baba body in 1973. Many people have reported that they have had Maharajji's darshan since then. Many people have seen Him in the form of Neem Karoli Baba. As stories tell of Maharajji's Lilas, He often came to people in other forms. It has been told that He could come as a dog, a child, as a soldier, and other forms. After He left the Neem Karoli Baba form, Maharajji continues to come to people using other forms. Maharajji also seems to speak through His devotees for limited times, of more or less than a minute or two. As we said, Maharajji is spirit or a super natural being. So, this is not surprising.

Gurudatji told this story to me in Vrindavan. "If you invited Maharajji to come to your home, He might come, but not in His usual form. A man invited Maharajji to a big party and Maharajji did not attend. When the man saw Maharajji again he said, 'Maharajji, why did you not come to my party?' Maharajji said, 'I did. I came as the dog. Why did you chase me away and turn me out of your home?' Then the man remembered that, on the night of the party, a dog had entered the yard and he had angrily chased it away with a stick. You never know what form Maharajji will take when He visits you."[21]

I believe we meet Maharajji in various forms throughout our lives. I feel that He comes to us at key moments and we do not necessarily recognize Him but he has an effect on us in the moment. He could be the beggar in the street asking for your help. In Hindu philosophy, the Guru can come to you in the form of a chiti (ant). When you see the whole world as Maharajji, everyone becomes an instrument of Maharajji. I think Maharajji likes to visit His children in different ways to "take a look at us" for His own reasons.

राम राम राम राम राम राम राम राम राम राम राम राम

Meeting Your Guru

Although they never met Maharajji in His body, many people often become devoted to Maharajji just by seeing His photo and without having much idea of who He is. This is a phenomenon that is little understood by anyone other than Maharajji. Remember, Maharajji was quoted as saying, "It is not necessary to meet your Guru on the physical plane. The Guru is not external."

"You've probably walked right by your Guru. She may have stopped you and given you a traffic ticket. You probably didn't even give him a quarter when he was asking for a handout. What do you know? Do you think the Guru's going to be someone with light streaming out, wearing a sandwich board sign that says, "I AM YOUR Guru"? When you're ready to see you'll see your Guru." - Ram Dass, Be Love Now[22]

राम राम राम राम राम राम राम राम राम राम राम राम

Maharajji's "Menu" for you is much larger than the menu within your mind. The apparent choices for the future are so much better than those of your own limited thinking. What Maharajji can deliver is so much greater.

Trust that Maharajji knows the plan for you..., that He will take care of it.

Faith and Belief: Proof is better. Maharajji proves He is there for you in any number of possible ways. The best faith to have is that Maharajji paves the road before you just as you take the step. Devotees can step into the unknown, unseen future with absolute confidence.

Maharajji said, "If you have enough faith you can give up money and possessions. God will give you everything you need for your spiritual development."

राम राम राम राम राम राम राम राम राम राम राम राम

Rabboo said, "One of the best parts of Maharajji's grace is that while you are experiencing it you know it's Maharajji's grace."

राम राम राम राम राम राम राम राम राम राम राम राम

You Have a Plan for Your Own Life

You formed the plan before you took this current birth. It could be called your karma. Upon birth, your parents began training you. In many cases, they trained your Jivatma's life plan right out of your conscious remembrance. They overlaid a nice straight middle class plan on top of you. Or maybe it's a lowly plan or an up-scale reality. They had plenty of help in taming you and getting you in line with what you are supposed to do. There are plenty of schools, religious organizations, peer groups, social organizations to "guide" you. Yet when you are older and there are feelings that something is not quite right, that you are off the mark, you couldn't quite put your finger on the problem. You are sort of doing their life plan for you, and there is something eating at you. Maybe you are very successful, but your wife and kids hate you, or your job isn't fulfilling, or maybe your life is utterly horrible and difficult and filled with bad luck. Or maybe everything is great in your life, but you know that you're getting older and one day your body will give out and die. At the core of the life plan we all have, is love. What we need to understand is that we enter the theater of life, play out the drama, and then leave only to return again with all that we have learned and experienced from the other incarnations. The confusion is caused by your mind. The closer you come to your Jivatma soul consciousness, to your field of love, the better you can understand the reality that you seek.

राम राम राम राम राम राम राम राम राम राम राम राम

You Are Never Alone

You are never "alone" when you belong to Maharajji. Maharajji is always with you. When you are with Maharajji, you are in the midst of a wonderful and interesting movie that is not within the psychological control of modern day media persuasion. This is why the powers that be (PTB) are constantly working on limiting your options to the sensory things of life. They want the limit of your life to be sense gratification brought about by their products of every type, including the non-stop media. At this time, the PTB will not recognize anything beyond a narrow doctrine, a very narrow system of realty. Realizing Maharajji is a way out of that box. It is the next step at this time – the next step in the growth of the human race.

Maharajji is bringing a more "real" reality. The body is carrying all sorts of cellular memory from ages upon ages. The reptile mind at the depths of your human mind exerts all sorts of pressures on your behavior. The DNA is carrying all sorts of consciousness. It is simply wrong to believe that is the extent of consciousness. Within the greater consciousness is the formed and the unformed – form and formless (focused on the physical plane and unfocused on the physical plane). Our consciousness extends beyond the physical. Who we are extends beyond the physical. In this awakening, we are beginning to more fully understand the true nature of reality – an expanded understanding of reality that is as profound as the difference between the way a Cro-Magnon being and a modern human perceive reality. The next step for us makes us more real. The science of Quantum Physics coming from the physical side of this is beginning to realize that the science used by Maharajji in His many forms is the same.

Consciousness

Humans have learned so much about the physical body all the way to the tiniest particles. Yet scientists have never found the soul, the Jivatma, which is who we are. So, these scientists believe that the Jivatma soul does not exist, because it is well beyond their ability to detect. This will never be found in physical-plane-based scientific research. The nature of consciousness cannot be discovered this way. It is a different science. Surely this is a science known to Maharajji.

Human science believes that our life consciousness resides in the brain, but this is not so. What Maharajji was doing is not brain-based. What Maharajji did was not, is not, brained-based. Maharajji did not use His brain to raise the dead, turn water into milk or petrol, make himself invisible, or make food appear out of nowhere.

राम राम राम राम राम राम राम राम राम राम राम राम

Where Human Consciousness Comes From

There are two basic beliefs in where human consciousness comes from:

Belief One:

You believe that atoms got together over a long timeframe and began to form more and more complex organisms that began to grow consciousness which evolved to self-aware human consciousness.

John Locke's "Essay Concerning Human Understanding," published in 1690, has often been cited as the origin of Western culture's concept of consciousness, defined as "the perception of what passes in one's own mind." Associated with what could be called this "Evolutionary Consciousness" are what Sigmund Freud proposed as a vertical, hierarchal structure of human consciousness with Conscious at top: Preconscious in middle and the Unconscious underlying all. What Freud believed was that important psychic events occurred below the surface and inside the unconscious mind. Freud further divided the Unconscious Mind into the Ego (who you think you are) and the Id, (instincts and drive).

Carl Jung also thought that personality was determined by the unconscious but he went a bit further and divided the unconscious into two layers: the personal unconscious (material once conscious but forgotten or repressed) and the collective unconscious (inherited psychic structures and archetypical experiences). Many scientists do not believe that the unconscious mind exists at all. In New Age circles there is a rough equivalent of the Unconscious called the Subconscious that proponents claim can be influenced subliminally.

Belief Two:

You believe that consciousness exists outside of the physical plane and indeed creates the physical plane. Consciousness uses the physical world as a playground. This could be called Cosmic Consciousness but it is beyond the physical world that contains the cosmic realm within it. We will refer to Atma as the Supreme consciousness and Jivatma as the individual consciousness in each of us.

The latter (Belief Two) is what Maharajji is, where Maharajji is coming from, and what Maharajji is working with. It took the scientific researchers of The Harvard Psychedelic Club to tell us about this, and to indeed subsequently open a door that allowed us to become aware of Maharajji. In particular, Dr. Richard Alpert (whom Maharajji named Ram Dass – Servant of God, or more literally Slave of God) followed an arduous path from this research to the lotus feet of Maharajji, who resided in a fully consciousness, fully realized state, in the foothills of the Himalayas.

Maharajji is a fully totally realized consciousness playing (doing Lila's) on the physical plane, while also remaining unattached to the physical plane.

राम राम राम राम राम राम राम राम राम राम राम राम

Individual Consciousness

Sometimes individual consciousness (Jivatma) is focused in a human body; and sometimes not focused (not appearing on the physical plane). We call the unfocused ones "dead." But they are not dead, as in non-existent. They are unfocused in bodies on the physical plane. They will be back, because these unfocused Jivatmas enjoy playing here, so they will focus into a body from time to time. We all do. This is the nature of reincarnation - the transmigration of souls.

"We must see that consciousness is neither an isolated soul nor the mere function of a single nervous system, but of that totality of interrelated stars and galaxies which makes a nervous system possible." - Alan Watts (1915 - 1973).

"I regard consciousness as fundamental. I regard matter as derivative from consciousness. We cannot get behind consciousness. Everything that we talk about, everything that we regard as existing, postulates consciousness." - Max Planck, Nobel Prize winning Physicist.[23]

"To say that the universe is participatory is to say that consciousness matters. But the conventional view, that we're just 'a pack of neurons' or 'computers made of meat,' or that 'we're all zombies,' as Crick, Minsky and Dennett assert, respectively, says otherwise. This view has no place for any meaningful degree of participation. This is an outdated perspective lodged in classical physics. It stems from the assumption that the brain's material particles and fields can give a full account of consciousness. But as physicist Stapp says, 'This [view] ... is motivated primarily by ideas about the natural world that have been known to be fundamentally incorrect for more than three-quarters of a century.'" – Dr. Larry Dossey.[24]

Your body does not have the limits, does not have the edges it appears to have. It is deeply affected by many other things, including all sorts of radio waves, and thought-waves and things such as the movement of heavenly bodies that we call astrology. These things are an extension of what appears to be your body, so to speak. They are part of the dance. So what your soul is "inhabiting" appears to have a defined form. And it indeed does on one level. But in the sense of the science of Maharajji, the being you are inhabits a plane of consciousness.

You are focused in the plane of consciousness and appearing as a human being in a human being's body. If you do not remember that you are more than this, then you are content to go about human life on a daily basis believing that you are simply a human born of molecules that will ultimately discorporate and fall apart. Game Over..., finished. And you're right. But it's over only for that form, only for that particular bodily you. The cells of that particular you, of course, were constantly regenerating and dying for your entire life anyway, so there is no specific "You" that you can hold onto. What's not "finished" is the You that is riding in that body. The real You just keeps rolling on.

राम राम राम राम राम राम राम राम राम राम राम राम

The Hologram Is All There Is

It seems that the greater consciousness creates the physical plane as a hologram. Maharajji can simply appear or disappear at will within that hologram. There is the seen hologram and the unseen hologram, within the physical plane, based on speed of motion and vibratory frequency. We can explain how holograms, as three dimensional images, can be created with laser, with light beams, etc., on the physical plane. But quite naturally the mechanism that the greater consciousness uses to create the hologram of the entire physical plane is and will evermore remain completely unknown to us. Yet scientific researchers are beginning to find evidence that our brains use holograms, as well.

राम राम राम राम राम राम राम राम राम राम राम राम

Consciousness Manipulates DNA

Consciousness manipulates DNA. In fact, consciousness created DNA. Are you beautiful? Your Jivatma consciousness created this. It's all part of your karma. Crooked teeth..., same. Short or very tall..., same. Blue eyes or brown eyes..., same. Ectomorph, Endomorph, Mesomorph..., same. Every single aspect of your body is created with material we call DNA (and more) that was created by Atma consciousness. The position of every planet at the moment of your birth was selected to help in the experience you are having, just as the DNA structure was chosen by Jivatma consciousness for that experience. What happens and when it happens is part of your individual "grand design." As Ram Dass[25] so rightly said, "There are no mistakes in this game." Nothing is random. You just don't see it correctly. As long as we are in the time and space of the physical plane we will never see it, or know it. But also, we don't actually need to know it or see it. We are wrapped within it.

Maharajji said that it is not right to teach by differences. Maharajji taught that it is "all one." We are ALL unique, but we are not so much different. DNA studies indicate that there is more diversity, more genetic differences in a group of African gorillas than in the entire human race. That seems to have been caused when something like 97% of the human race was killed by what may have been a huge asteroid collision with Earth. The difference between brown eyes and blue eyes seems to be one gene. If the gene is in the off position, eyes are brown, and if in the on position eyes are blue – other color differences being caused by the chemical nature of the body.

राम राम राम राम राम राम राम राम राम राम राम राम

You Are God

You are already God, within you. It really is not a matter of perfecting yourself to earn points to either take a new birth or to not take a new birth. It is a matter of you deciding. That is, once you are at a certain point. I believe that those who *pranam* to Maharajji, who deeply love Maharajji, who serve Maharajji are at that point. There is absolutely no higher authority than your own Jivatma, an actual part of Atma, God, the Divine. None, nada, zilch, zero.

Maharajji is Atma, and you, as Jivatma, are part of Atma. It is a matter of your level of realization while you are within your body. Maharajji is what is called the fully realized being. There are billions who appear to be barely realized beings who have not bridged the gap between mind and the inner goodness of Jivatma. With the requisite stimulus, illusions are stripped away and a ray of light, a glimmer of understanding, can come to all.

God was not "invented" by the human mind. God was "discovered" by the human mind. And it took a lot of effort by a lot of very special souls to strip away the illusion, to see and feel the effects of God in the world, the consciousness we call God. The old Babas in the caves worked and worked to go to the deepest level within themselves to find the truth. When Jesus said, "I am the way, the truth and the light," he was coming from his Jivatma soul and when he said "I" and you say "I" it is the same "I." All of us are God.

Maybe this realization comes from a Near Death Experience (NDE), or from taking a psychotropic, or many years of spiritual practice such as yoga or meditation, or a long illness, or any other thing that triggers your body to relinquish its hold on your mind long enough to realize the utterly benign and loving consciousness within. The first step of realization begins with understanding who "you" are. That is the first step on the "Spiritual Path"…, to begin to see who "I" is.

राम राम राम राम राम राम राम राम राम राम राम राम

This beautiful expression is Baba Ram Dass' definition of *Namaste*: "I honor that place in you, when you are in that place in you and I am in that place in me, there is only one of us." Indeed, there really is only one of us. This is not a projection or exercise of our mind. To experience it, you must move your mind out of the way, so you can get to the reality of this.

राम राम राम राम राम राम राम राम राम राम राम राम

Jivatma Is Not Subservient

Jivatma is not a subservient "thing." Your Jivatma is a "piece" of God. Atma is God. Jivatma is an aspect of God. You are God consciousness riding in a human body. The "spark" of your life is God. What leaves your body when you die is, again, a piece of God. You have the ultimate say as to life's experiences. The thing that is subservient is actually the body, although the body/mind constantly thinks and feels that it is the decision-maker, that it has some control in the "big picture." Not so. Those who extricate themselves from the illusion that the body is all there is, and is the sum total of your human experience, can attest to that. But this isn't something that everyone always talks about. It is something that is the result of an inner awakening so this generally isn't something that is trumpeted about. Those around you may see the "struggle" you are going through as you begin your spiritual path to finding that the "You" within you is not the same you that you thought you were. Yet they can't see what is going on inside you, as the lotus flower of realization opens within you..

राम राम राम राम राम राम राम राम राम राम राम राम

Karma and Reincarnation (Transmigration of Souls)

Historical scholars see karma and reincarnation (transmigration of souls) differently and virtually none of them understand enough about it. It seems that a long time ago, back in the time of the *Vedas*[26], they were studying how they could remain in good standing so that they could take the next birth. Now, some 4,500-6,000 years later, it seems to have reversed and people talk about remaining in good standing so that they can escape the wheel of births and deaths. Maybe the whole process has accelerated and there is a different way that Jivatma sees the process. Let Maharajji teach you what these things mean by both inner and outer guidance.

"Whether or not you believe in reincarnation does not affect the fact of reincarnation one iota."[27] None of this was "invented" by the human mind. It was however "discovered" by the human mind. Yet the human mind is running wild on Earth. It has been running wild for thousands of years and it's getting wilder all the time. All around you, you see the effects of the human mind gone wild. Yet, the mind is still not enough to win the battle between real truth and lies. Every single human being carries the truth within their Jivatma. And this is realized in varying degrees.

Most people don't think much about or remember their other lives, but they frequently access skills from other lives without ever knowing it. Maybe you were a skilled tailor in another life and in this life occasionally draw on that experience for seeing things in this life. Exceptional cooks in the middle-class home may have had other lives as well-trained chefs for the royalty, nobility, and elites in other lives. Like that. It takes a lot of extra work to actively remember even one of your other lives. All of us can get a faint inkling of them sometimes. To go deeper with this, often one must do what is called a "Past Life Regression," and there are trained practitioners that can help you. One is truly graced to be able to receive the power of the conscious knowing of the role one played in one's other lives.

I feel that the reason most people, when they are younger, believe they will live forever is that they receive an inner message from their Jivatma because it is immortal, but the "I" that thinks it will live forever in not the real "I." It is the mind tricking you into thinking that your body will not get old and die. Yet if you realize you are your Jivatma, you instantly realize that it all just keeps going round and round. And that's okay, isn't it? That's the next discovery by the human race.

राम राम राम राम राम राम राम राम राम राम राम राम

Karma Is Your Course of Study

Your overall karma is your course of study. Your course of study covers everything. It was implied by scholars that karma was invented by the powers that be to control people, to force them to be good so that they would not pick up bad karma from actions in this life. Sure, there is an element of this. But really in all your many life's roles as everything from the cruel king to the trod upon peasant, the killer and the killed, the winner and the loser, the horrible life of being possessed by demons and the life of near bliss in heavenly comfort, the healer and the one who is healed, the life with a virtually perfect body and the life with a twisted malfunctioning body, you are just acting in a play that you agreed to play out long before you took the first of these births.

Your human you does not have dominion and ever-lasting life, but your Jivatma does. It just depends on who you think you are. There is no timeline except in the illusion of the physical plane. To your greater Jivatma soul, it is all happening outside of time, it is only within the physical plane that the Jivatma can experience time. The more your illusions of separateness are moved out of the way, the more you experience the bliss of the ride in the physical plane and can pass this on to others, as well as deeply sharing the deepest togetherness possible.

राम राम राम राम राम राम राम राम राम राम राम राम

Incarnations

Do we know all these other people around us? Are we constantly meeting people who we have known from other lives? Yes. In the years that my life has revolved around Maharajji, I have realized that all these people are beings known to me in some long-term multi-life way. It is not readily apparent "who" they are but I know them, and they know me. We do this dance over and over again, each playing our roles so perfectly. Occasionally the connection and the knowing is very deep. There are beings that are instantly recognized from other lives. It is one of the great mysteries that we are not more capable of piercing the veil that is between our incarnations.

In the West, people seem to think that reincarnation means that, if you're bad, you'll come back as a chicken or some such nonsense. Not really. That's what my grade school teacher told us when we were studying different religions and it seems to be a recurring theme in the thinking of non-Hindus even when they are much older. Generally, the Jivatma has free will to plan whatever is required of the "next" life. And also, the Jivatma is not evolving backwards, ever. It is always growing in its perception of the physical plane. All of "us" are growing and learning on the path to being fully realized beings on the physical plane. Your soul is an incarnation that has experienced much in other lives, and part of the game in this play is to get better and better. Yet your Jivatma consciousness could take birth within a tree, as its vehicle. A very meditative life, I imagine. Or you could try stuffing your huge Jivatma consciousness into the body of a chicken for a couple of months. That's all the time you'll have in one of those bodies in this day and age.

According to Maharajji, rebirth can sometimes be about desire. "If you desire a mango at the moment of death, you'll be born an insect. If you even desire the next breath, you will take birth again." This is one of the quotes of Maharajji that I have reflected on for many years and have come to realize that this quote is likely out of context. Your karmic destiny can be affected by a desire at the time of your leaving your body, yet the game is bigger than that.

I feel that Maharajji, as my Guru, has guided me away from thinking that our journey through so many incarnations is determined by a split second at the moment of death of the body. This is much more about ceasing to desire than it is about how you "line up" on your next birth. However, if at the moment of your death you desire nothing more than to be with Maharajji, this will surely happen. I am quite sure that this quote is a teaching given to one individual devotee. Jivatma do not devolve. Jivatma always grow with every life's experience. This, of course, is not a linear experience. Jivatma is not in time and space, but focuses on apparent time and space to experience time and space on the physical plane. The desire of the Jivatma and the desire of your animal body are not the same. The apparent struggle is between the multi-life consciousness of your Jivatma and the chemically controlled animal consciousness of the body.

रामराम राम राम राम राम राम राम राम राम राम राम

One of the best aspects of what we call death is that you (your Jivatma) instantly returns to being a fully realized all knowing consciousness. You know every aspect of the life you just came out of, as well as everyone you met in that life, and also all the other life manifestations you have had, ever.

It is a tremendous stretch for your consciousness to be an American in an Asian city in India, China, Thailand, Viet Nam, etc., watching thousands of people all around and seeing that they are all you at heart. They seem so different, yet they are you. There is no difference except superficial physical plane appearances, some cultural training and their own temperament.

In "The Seth Material"[28], Jane Roberts channeled the analogy of our lives as a multitrack sound recorder where each track contained a different instrument – bass, drums, lead guitar, rhythm guitar, keyboard, lead singer, background singer. They are all separate and individually controllable when separated like this. But when they are mixed in and they are added together, you can experience the whole song. In much the same way, our own various incarnations are separated. It takes work on our part to pierce this veil and realize aspects of these other incarnations in some way.

In "Autobiography of a Yogi"[29], Swami Yogananda tells of how, in 1861 near Ranikhet, his Guru's Guru, Lahiri Mahasaya, met Mahavatar Babaji in the cave in the mountains. Babaji told him that he had been with them living in that same cave when his previous body had died. Babaji showed him his place in the cave with all of his things just as he had left it. Suddenly Lahiriji remembered everything. Lahiri later returned to Varanasi, where he began initiating sincere seekers into the path of *Kriya Yoga*[30]. Lahiriji is the epitome of the perfect householder Guru. It must be noted that there is a story that says Mahavatar Babaji, like Neem Karoli Baba, is also one of the manifestations of Maharajji.

राम राम राम राम राम राम राम राम राम राम राम राम

Transmigrational Amnesia

That we do not remember these former lives or indeed future lives is transmigrational amnesia. The body that our Jivatma soul comes into at birth is so strong that it overrides our memories of other lives. When the baby is born, it knows all about the other lives and particularly the life of the body it just left in the timeline, but the forces of their new body and the training of family and society completely subdue this knowing until it becomes but a vague dream. The baby knows more about this than the parents. Yet the baby buries the remembering and forgets. The baby joins the parents and the whole family in the experience of this life unhampered by confusion with other lives.

After we leave these current lives, when we are reborn, we come back with amnesia. We remember some things from the past, by the time we (in our new bodies) are capable of "normal" adult functioning in the world, our remembrances of our former lives are buried. I feel that Maharajji placed murtis in so many temples because we could use them to remember our other lives with Maharajji and to realize the connection we have with Him. It also provides a place where we can gather together with people we have known from other lives. Often at the feet of a Hanuman murti or Maharajji's tucket we can remember things that we don't easily remember from our other lives.

Over the years, I've often heard how people, particularly Americans, who bring their young children to Sri Taos Hanumanji remark that their child seems to know how to behave in the temple room without being instructed. They are, of course, kids so this is very subtle and the parents may catch only a glimpse of this behavior. For the adults and young adults it will likely take quite a bit of time and many hours of practice to remember having done this all before. Welcome home. We are so glad you have been reunited with your family who gathers around Maharajji in many lifetimes.

Yet, the knowing of past lives (and future lives) is still available to one who does their work to get to them. It all resides in the Jivatma, in your soul. The more you get your animal consciousness out of the way the better. If it is not your karma to open enough to break out of the illusion of the new life, then you can go through the whole of the new life with no idea about any of this. Yet it is the actual reality of what is happening.

राम राम राम राम राम राम राम राम राम राम राम राम

Transitory Worldly Attachment

The things of the world are not satisfying by any means, because they are completely   transitory. Whatever we may have acquired or consumed is but further attachment that keeps us running around in circles. You always ultimately become bored with the sameness of the things you are chasing. And in most ways you are indeed a prisoner to this. It is not that there is anything wrong with the experience of human life in modern times. It is indeed why we took birth. The problem is that this does not lead anywhere. So often rich people are asking, "Is this all there is?" "Where are we all going?" We are going to our death and soaking up everything we can along the way. That's okay.

When we are not in our bodies (unfocused on the physical plane) we are transitioning to our next physical plane life. The question in your current life is more about You, about your sense of well being. What you must play out in this life is essentially your karma. But don't be confused about karma. Karma goes hand in hand with transmigration of souls (reincarnation). In the many lives a Jivatma lives on the physical plane, it will experience everything - riches, poverty, health, illness, pleasure, pain, power, exploitation, bravery, cowardice, ecstatic states, mundane states, intense love, intense hatred, being a leader, being a follower, knowing, and not having a clue, are all part of this multi-life experience.

Either you have the power to know or you don't know. That isn't meaning intelligence, for that is a function of the body's mind (brain). Your mind has either gotten connected enough to your Jivatma that you remain connected to the bigger picture, or it hasn't. If you're connected, then you know. As much as you may appear to be in poverty in this life you are in riches in another life. Being caught up in the attachment of your current life can cut you off from the realization that you are always the same at the core of all of your lives. Although, it is perfectly fine to focus intensely on your current life as you be here now. You are the consciousness that is riding in your body to experience the physical plane in all its dimensions. Each Jivatma life is equal. That is what was so marvelous about what the founders of the United States knew and indeed taught to the world.

Each Life "Scores" a One

Each life is simply a "1." It has no greater or lesser value than "1." From the Jivatma standpoint a life of 2 years is equal to a life of 100 years. When you leave your body, you receive another 1 on your scoreboard (this is, of course, a metaphor). No more, no less. All that is in between your birth and your death is a sort of illusion, so you might as well enjoy it and see it for what it is. Humans are more and more beginning to see this and to realize that rather than "life after death;" there is "life after life." It is the animal part of us that is deluded.

It is the DNA side that has the hold on us. It tries everything to override the Jivatma and convince you that the physical plane reality is the only reality for consciousness. Yet this is simply not true. The truth is that your ongoing soul is so much more than that. Our Jivatmas are dancing in the DNA, but Jivatma is not controlled by our DNA.

Atma (the collective greater consciousness) created DNA as part of the way our bodies were created as vehicles for our Jivatma individual soul consciousness. And Atma continues to change the physical world to accommodate for the time ahead.

Why Do We Take Birth"?

Why are we living? Why do we take yet another Birth"? So that our Jivatma can soak up all the experiences of our life in this particular body that we are in right now. We are learning from each incarnation. Time is on a linear scale. It's real and not real. Yet, our karmas, attached to our Jivatma, are not necessarily "earned" as much as they are "selected." Karma is a course in learning on the physical plane throughout many lifetimes. We are in the middle of time, always. That is to say that our lives in the future stretching out in front of us are as "real" as our past lives stretching out behind us. There seems to be some time impeller that creates the existence of time on physical lives. The point is that we're learning in every life so that these things are improving us all the time. Consciousness is now creating this new reality on Earth as never before. Over a period of tens of thousands of years, in both time directions from the here and now, consciousness is learning how to do things that are very helpful to future human beings. We, as a whole, are now beginning to understand how the world works and recognizing how best we can all live in peaceful, prosperous ways.

We like to be in the illusion of our own immortality for a little while. That's okay. It is all part of the dance. Why think about death all the time? It's not necessary. Yet reality is different. Near the end of our lives as the body begins to fail, no matter how robust and powerful we once were, we seek the truth. Everyone does.

राम राम राम राम राम राम राम राम राम राम राम राम

Life Is Experiential

You are here for the experience of living this particular life. Your life's experience can be repetitive and boring, or diverse, informative and exciting. While it would appear that all life experiences are external, that they are "worldly," there are many experiences that are strictly internal and within the body. All life experiences are OK, because they are the life experience each of us elected, and that represent our karma.

A philosopher remarked that every being on Earth is the exact center of the conscious universe – every human, every animal, and every insect – and asked, "Isn't that amazing?" All are having an "experience." All are looking outward at it all.[31]

राम राम राम राम राम राम राम राम राम राम राम राम

Opening of Consciousness

Getting your body-mind under control is a huge task. That is not to say that making the body physically fit and especially strong or long-lived is the task. Our bodies are controlled by so many chemicals, not the least are estrogen and testosterone, that drive the human bodies often far beyond any rational control by our Jivatma souls. Most people are like "sitting ducks" for these chemicals to control us. There are a lot more chemicals in the body that hold us but they are not what we are focusing on here.

Mostly the realization of who Maharajji is happens when there is an "opening" in these chemicals either by the chemicals subsiding long enough that your mind realizes that there is something greater going on, or by taking an overriding psychotropic chemical - LSD, Mescaline, etc., as well as to a lesser extent Marijuana herb. These chemicals are not affecting the perspective of Jivatma at all because Jivatma is eternal and unchanged by physical plane forces. These chemicals in the body are getting in the way of your perception of Jivatma - the Jivatma being a rider in your body. Through such experimentation, it can be understood that the body is a vehicle.

राम राम राम राम राम राम राम राम राम राम राम राम

Maharajji said that smoking *charas* (hashish) or *ganja* (marijuana bud) or eating *bhang (ingested marijuana)* was okay. There is a story told to me by a Westerner that is not in any of the books about Maharajji. It tells of a day when there were lots of young Westerners staying in the ashram. Maharajji called from His tucket to have everyone bring ALL the hashish they had to him. They dared not hold back or hide any of it because Maharajji knows everything. They brought a huge amount – several softball size balls, thumb size, little finger size, little strands like spaghetti, as well as patties, etc.. Wow. Kids will be kids. Maharajji then redistributed these saying to some people "do not smoke" anymore. To some people he said, you should try smoking a little of this. He gave the softball size pieces to some old *chillum*[32] baba sadhus there. He was like a doctor dispensing herbal medicines.

The Marijuana products are only a very mild form of consciousness shifting substance. The following description of Indian's perspective tells where the ancient practice of using marijuana as a sacrament comes from "...because of its association with the religious life of the country that bhang is so extolled and glorified. The stupefaction produced by the plant's resin is greatly valued by the fakirs and ascetics, the holy men of India, because they believe that communication with their deities is greatly facilitated during intoxication with bhang. (According to one legend, the Buddha subsisted on a daily ration of one cannabis seed, and nothing else, during his six years of asceticism.) Taken in early morning, the drug is believed to cleanse the body of sin. Like the communion of Christianity, the devotee who partakes of bhang partakes of the god Siva."[33]

Did LSD Open the Door?

The real psychotropics can take one to the point where the walls melt and the body can totally disappear. Many of the Western people who "realized" Maharajji and had the darshan of Maharajji had taken LSD as a first step in opening themselves to even the possibility of who Maharajji is. This was because in Western culture there is simply no basis for the belief in the existence of a being like Maharajji.

Did LSD open the door to Maharajji? Was there something about the universal consciousness brought about by ingesting LSD that allowed Maharajji to see us and to know that we are ready? Maharajji pulled Ram Dass to Him in a most remote area of the mountains of India. Ram Dass was the perfect person to bring information about Maharajji back to America and the Sixties was the perfect time. I believe that Ram Dass was the most important person to ever speak to the public in America. Ram Dass brought the message of Maharajji to America..., and permanently changed the consciousness of Western culture. Ram Dass said that before LSD, people believed everything was "real," but afterwards people began to realize that things could be "relatively real."

Gurudat Sharma (Maharajji's *pandit*) was there with Maharajji when Ram Dass was first brought to Him and he was there 72 days later when Ram Dass left. He said the transformation in Ram Dass during that time was immense. Ram Dass returned to the USA and began to speak to people about his experiences. Many times Ram Dass was recorded while speaking. These recordings were transcribed and ultimately were used to make the book, "Be Here Now." It is a journey through consciousness. It is particularly important in understanding how consciousness plays into the lives of many of us. If your consciousness is ready for the information in "Be Here Now," it fills you as though you had drunk thousands of liters of pure life-giving water.

One day at Lama Foundation[34], Ram Dass told me that he didn't write the book, that Maharajji wrote "Be Here Now." "Be Here Now" just happened. It was all Maharajji's Lila. It seems that with "Be Here Now," Maharajji channeled it through Ram Dass. It seems to have happened the way all Lilas of Maharajji happen. They are not born from or carried out with a rational thought process. Various elements that otherwise would not have been moved to participate simply do what is necessary to cause it to manifest, as though guided by a singular unseen force. That such a book would be made in such a way at Lama Foundation near the tiny New Mexico village of San Cristobal, and that it would go on to sell millions of copies worldwide, is an absolute marvel. Yet that is what happened. There was and still is a global awakening of consciousness. It is the realization of a consciousness beyond normal waking consciousness.

राम राम राम राम राम राम राम राम राम राम राम राम

Gurudat Sharma told me that, when he was young, he and a group of other young men would be with Maharajji through the night. Whenever these devotees began to fall asleep Maharajji would not allow them to sleep. Then when the sun began to rise, Maharajji would say, "OK, you can go to sleep now." They would say with much laughter, "Maharajji, how can we go to sleep? The sun is rising." They were never tired after staying awake all night with Maharajji.

राम राम राम राम राम राम राम राम राम राम राम राम

Human Mind

The mind is a great slave but a terrible master. Your Jivatma consciousness is in a body on the physical plane and your body has a mind. This mind is not to be "shut down;" it is to be used and to be tamed. It can be used simply for thinking and it can be used for a lot more than that. It is a marvelous tool capable of amazing feats, but the mind has created much havoc in the world through wrong thinking.

The mind is imperfect, as we all know. It comes with a basic operating system and certain abilities. Then it is additionally programmed as our body grows, as you observe and interact with the world around you, and as you are programmed by others (taught). The knowing of the Jivatma is perfect, but the knowing of the mind is not perfect and can never be perfect. The mind can be honed and it can have amazing thought capabilities in specific areas for decades. Yet the mind can be fooled, it can be led to believe outright lies, it can be psychologically controlled, it can forget important things, it can be completely ignorant of important facts, and it is the mind that can prematurely close accounts with the true nature of reality. Wrong thinking of the mind unnecessarily creates all sorts of dramas for many people.

The mind seems to think that it knows everything, but it does not and cannot know everything. Of course, You know everything, but it is not your mind that is doing the knowing. It is only your Jivatma riding within your body that knows everything..., literally everything. Your mind is actually limiting you. When Jivatma controls mind, the result is better for you and for all around you.

राम राम राम राम राम राम राम राम राम राम राम राम

Maharajji seems to have "cracked" the minds of devotees on many occasions. The minds of the devotees just could not comprehend their observance of these Lilas of Maharajji as described in so many stories. These Lilas certainly moved devotees to "think outside the box" in so many ways, and most assuredly points to a higher power than the mind. These Lilas begin to alert devotees to their Jivatma.

There is a little story from "By His Grace: A Devotee's Story" that is one of those that would deeply affect the people seeing it unfold. "We were sitting with Maharajji near the front of the ashram when a sadhu came walking in the gate. He had a big *jata* and a beard, was wearing *rudhraksha* beads and carrying a trident. As soon as he saw the man, Babaji jumped up and ran toward him. Babaji met the man, spoke to him for a minute or two, and then the man disappeared. He just disappeared! Usha Bahadur cried, 'Who was that person?' Maharajji never said a word about it."[35]

The spine, which of course is an extension of the mind, controls most rote functioning that humans do. If you are playing music, or driving a car, or competing in a sport, you are using what has been programmed into your spine. Your mind has trained your spine to perform in certain ways. That is the reason one engages in practice and training.

But the Mind can do so much more than think. As we know, correctly used, the mind has the power to change things. The human mind has a reach that goes beyond the body. The purpose of this book is not to describe the wonderment and functions of the mind, however, because what we are discovering herein is that which is beyond the mind. If you want to play with the capabilities of your mind there are ample means of discovery in this world. A mind that is controlled by the Jivatma soul is indeed a wonderment of power. Get your own mind out of the way, get your mind under control, and you will know the real power of Jivatma.

राम राम राम राम राम राम राम राम राम राम राम राम

Truth

Maharajji always guided people to program their minds with "the truth." An element of this truth is simply right thinking about daily mundane actions, because thinking is mostly about what we say and do throughout the course of the day. The truth goes beyond "common thinking." The basic truth is that You are not your mind. You are your Jivatma.

Maharajji said, "Truth is the most difficult tapasya. Men will hate you for telling the truth. They will call you names. They may even kill you, but you must tell the truth. If you live in truth, God will always stand with you."

Truth on the physical plane is not so easy to know. To speak the truth often means that in your speaking you should not deceive people. Sometimes the truth is not what it appears initially, and much effort must be made to get to the truth. You may not know the full truth, but you must always seek the truth before you start telling truth to everyone. Often knowing only a half-truth creates problems for everyone. The mind might say, "This is truth," but you cannot fully trust your mind. You must look deep within and often you must wait for the truth to fully unfold before you. The study of truth could fill volumes of books. There are the small truths of the physical plane mind and the greater truth of the Jivatma soul consciousness.

राम राम राम राम राम राम राम राम राम राम राम राम

Maharajji said, "Total truth is necessary. You must live by what you say."

राम राम राम राम राम राम राम राम राम राम राम राम

There Is Apparent Chaos

In the physical world there is apparent chaos. Bearing in mind that consciousness created the physical plane, with its constantly changing name (nama) and form (rupa), from a place, removed from the physical plane, a place of "*sat*" [essential being – Jivatma], of "*chit*" [essential consciousness – Atma], and of "ananda" [Bliss beyond bliss]..., consciousness actually controls the physical world.

As previously written, the physical plane can be perceived as a hologram. An understanding of this is not new by any means. The physical world is a holographic "reality" controlled by a universal consciousness that is in fact well beyond the physical world. Those in the fields of quantum physics are increasingly discovering the truth of these things.

There are patterns in everything – much more order than even the smartest, best trained humans realize. Increasingly, as quantum physicists search the unknown, they are arriving at an understanding that is the same knowing of the highest holy men in the caves of the Himalayas. Maharajji is using the science of both apparent sides of this.

There is much more order in our individual human life as well, even though you feel that it might be chaotic. The makers of the products you buy may claim that the product will make you stand apart from others (differentiate) but that is just a sales pitch. Still, if you want to be brand conscious, no problem. Just remember that it means little and don't get attached.

Yet Maharajji showed many of His devotees that things are not always what we "think" they are. Maharajji is about higher truth. Maharajji upbraided people because they weren't "thinking" about their tasks, but Maharajji essentially told people not to think when it came to the higher truths, that you would become crazy if you tried to figure it all out.

राम राम राम राम राम राम राम राम राम राम राम राम

"What Maharajji wants us to do is look inside ourselves and find Him there. Once we make that internal spiritual connection with Maharajji, we will never be apart from Him ever again."[36]

It's All Maharajji

Maharajji Raised the Dead

This story is so subtle. "Babaji was in the habit of visiting a nearby village. One evening he came to the house of a devotee where he often took his food. The lady of the house came out crying bitterly and said, 'The person who used to serve you your food is lying there.' He lay dead, surrounded by the people who had come to arrange for his cremation. Babaji sat down by the man, put a part of his blanket over the man's body, and began talking to the people around him. Everyone was looking at Babaji and listening to him. After some time, Babaji got up and said he would go and take his food somewhere else. No one thought of stopping him. After Baba had gone away, the man lying there sat up as if from sleep and asked, 'Why am I lying here?' Everyone was so dazed that no one could reply."[37]

राम राम राम राम राम राम राम राम राम राम राम राम

I heard the following story in Vrindavan about a year before Yudhisthir Singh left his body. The story happened when Yudhisthir was quite young, many years before.

Maharajji was on the plains of India. He told Yudhisthir to come along with Him to the mountains. Yudhisthir told Maharajji that he had just taken driver training and now had a driving license, so he could help with driving duties. Maharajji said, "No. If Yudhisthir drives we will all be killed."

The drive was very long but Maharajji would not let the driver stop to rest or take tea. The driver became so weary that he was just about passing out at the wheel. When they finally reached the mountains, Maharajji told Yudhisthir to drive, so he took the wheel. Remember, Yudhisthir had just recently learned to drive.

The road through the steep mountains to Maharajji's Bhumiadar Temple is extremely winding with a very deep drop-off on the side. Yudhisthir was petrified with fear so he was driving very slowly; something like 10-15 KMH. Yudhisthir was remembering that Maharajji said that if he drove they would all be killed. On top of that, Maharajji kept yelling at Yudhisthir to go faster.

After more than an hour of driving, they arrived at Bhumiadar in the evening. Maharajji withdrew to His room. Yudhisthir was a wreck after his harrowing drive, so he took food and immediately went to sleep on a mat on the pavement of one of the out-of-the-way temple areas.

During the night, a black snake bit Yudhisthir, and Yudhisthir turned black, and he died. During the night the people at the temple noticed what had happened to

Yudhisthir and realized that he was dead. So they cleaned him up for cremation and put flowers on him.

In the morning Maharajji came out of His room, and asked what was going on with Yudhisthir. He was told that Yudhisthir was dead. Maharajji said, "No, he is not dead." Maharajji walked over to Yudhisthir and kicked him yelling "Get up." The temple staff helped Yudhisthir get up. Maharajji then told them to give him *chai*. Later Maharajji made Yudhisthir drive Him all the way to Ranikhet.

राम राम राम राम राम राम राम राम राम राम राम राम

Maharajji Was in Two Places at Once

One day I was hanging out in Vrindavan Ashram with Maharajji's son-in-law Jagdish. I said, "It must have been amazing having Maharajji as your father-in-law." He held up his open hand and said, "I saw Maharajji only once and that was for only ten minutes." He then narrated this story to me. In India, after the parents have arranged a marriage, there is a ceremony where the bribe and groom meet for the first time. The ceremony is the presenting of the goddess Lakshmi to Lord Vishnu. The families were waiting for Maharajji before this rite, at a house in Agra. Maharajji arrived in a car, entered the house, presented Girija to Jagdish, and then left in the car 10 minutes after arriving. That was the extent of his time with Maharajji. It was only later that Jagdish came to know the truth of who

Maharajji really is. Girija, of course, saw her father from time to time and brought their son Sandeep as a baby to Maharajji. Maharajji told her that Sandeep would be a pilot. In fact, later he did become a pilot with the Indian Air Force, flying MIGs. Jagdish is now a practitioner of Advaita[38] philosophy of non-dualism. I was amazed by this story and told this to Jagdish. He said, "Oh, this is not the amazing part of the story. The amazing part is that at the time of this event Maharajji was known to have been in Kainchi." This is among the least known of the "being in two places at once" stories.

राम राम राम राम राम राम राम राम राम राम राम राम

Luckily for all of us, the advent of widespread telephone service helped satsang catch Maharajji in many of His acts.

As another story tells, at the time of one Hindu holiday, devotees in Allahabad and Kanpur were speaking on the phone and the devotee in Kanpur described the bhandara and said that Maharajji was there. The devotee in Allahabad said that was impossible because Maharajji was there in His room.

The science of how Maharajji was able to do this is unknown to us. Was this astral travel? Did Maharajji go out of one body and appear in another body elsewhere? It could be as simple as that, but I don't think so. Is

Maharajji conscious in several bodies simultaneously? Really, it matters little. It's beyond that. Is this an example of some sort of time travel? It seems that Maharajji had several bodies. How can that be remotely possible for Maharajji to have more than one body? Again, that is something unknown to our time.

राम राम राम राम राम राम राम राम राम राम राम राम

Is Maharajji a time traveler using non-temporal time? Technically there is no past, present or future in the transmigration of souls. This is because there is no time and there is no space. Part of the science of Maharajji is the realization of this. I believe it is possible to time travel if you know that time isn't real and have found how to step out of time. Time travel may be easier using inner consciousness than by using some time-machine that actually doesn't exist yet. Appearing in two or more places at the same time is probably really a form of this time travel using the holographic nature of the physical plane. There are ample stories that this is the case with Maharajji.

राम राम राम राम राम राम राम राम राम राम राम राम

Asking Maharajji

Asking Maharajji, beseeching Maharajji, demanding of Maharajji, begging Maharajji, these are all possible. If you have a problem, simply ask Maharajji to solve it. Give your problem to Maharajji. He cannot refuse you. He is your Guru and it is His job to deal with your problem. You will no longer have to worry about the problem, but of course you cannot be attached to the exact outcome.

A person who is ill must simply ask Maharajji to heal them. Maharajji will find the best path to the best outcome of the disease. Even in the case of a person who is destined to die of the illness, the path is made better. So many of Maharajji's older devotees had their lives lengthened by many years because Maharajji held off their fatal diseases. Many Indian and American devotees of Maharajji were literally "brought back from death's door" and lived many years longer. Shivaya Baba was a person with immense devotion to Maharajji who lived ten years after a devastating health problem. He attributed his ten-year extension to Maharajji, as did we all.

In the case of my wife Radha's death from cancer, Maharajji seems to have eased Radha's pain. I immersed Radha's ashes into the Yamuna River in Vrindavan. In the party that accompanied me to Jumna-ji (Yamuna River) were Maharajji's son, Dharma Narayanji, Gurudatji, Radha's brother John, panditji, pujari, Western devotees Krishna and Satrupa, as well as Gopal Prasad Singh, our driver. After we had returned to Maharajji's ashram and were taking tea, Gurudat Sharmaji said, "I suppose that Radha was not having the same pain as other people who have experienced this disease. Maharajji took her pain." I thought about it a lot and had to admit that surely Maharajji drastically mitigated Radha's pain. For two years, this is something that I had been literally begging Maharajji to grant to Radha.

राम राम राम राम राम राम राम राम राम राम राम राम

Kehar "Papa" Singh was such a devotee. Maharajji cured/saved Papa Singh from so many dire ailments. As described in the book "Prem Avatar," "Babaji embracing Kehar Singhji and by rubbing his head 6-7 times with His hand got him rid of the tongue cancer. He once cured the swelling on his feet (caused by blood turning to water under the skin) by pressing on a certain point with his finger. Babaji gave eye-sight to his son whose eye was injured by the broken glass of his spectacles. Twenty-two pieces of glass had pierced his eye and had so damaged it that he became blind and many doctors failed to treat him. Babaji gave him eye-sight by simply pressing on a certain point in his (boy's) palm with His finger. He cured many by sending a flower only."[39]

Besides mitigating the illnesses of His devotees, there are many stories about how Maharajji pulled diseases out of people and took the disease into His own body. Maharajji would literally cure the person by taking the disease. It has sometimes been mentioned that the Indian devotees who were with Maharajji think that Maharajji's body would have lived much longer if He had not caused his body to be subjected to such diseases. After many years of contemplating this, I don't think so. Maharajji's play is beyond any such speculation. He cured and caused to be cured an untold number of persons' bodies of all manner of illnesses.

राम राम राम राम राम राम राम राम राम राम राम राम

One day many devotees were thanking Maharajji for saving them from dire circumstances. Maharajji asked if they believed He had the power to save them from the problem, didn't He also have the power to create the problem in the first place?

You can demand of Maharajji. You can pray to Maharajji. Often results require some sort of action on your part to begin. As Lao Tsu[40] said, "A journey of 10,000 miles begins with one step." If you take the first step, Maharajji often handles the rest. You must listen for the first step that Maharajji is telling you to take. It can be as simple as going to the chemist and buying an over-the-counter medicine, or sending out your resume.

Some devotees never ever ask Maharajji for anything. These devotees feel that Maharajji knows everything within their minds and all of their karma. They feel it is ridiculous to ask Maharajji to fulfill some desire, because they know Maharajji will do what is best for them and it is simply not necessary to pray to Him for personal things. Yet, asking Maharajji cannot be wrong. So often the whole satsang prays for Maharajji to heal the illnesses of devotees.

If you have asked Maharajji for an opportunity, now you must recognize the opportunity when it is presented. You must not think about it. Put Maharajji first. Put the mind second. We know that the mind is a great servant but a lousy master. I always ask Maharajji to make His directions so clear that even a dummy like me can understand. You are a child of Maharajji. He is not limited like your birth parents. You must listen to him and act accordingly.

राम राम राम राम राम राम राम राम राम राम राम राम

You may not want to ask Maharajji for a practice because He just might give you one. Coloni Walla Baba asked Maharajji for a practice. So Maharajji drew a four-foot circle on the ground and told Coloni Walla Baba that the practice was to stay in the circle until Maharajji returned. Maharajji pointed to one side and said that he could go over there to get water and pointed to the opposite direction and told him that he could go there for toilet. Then Maharajji went away. Coloni Walla Baba said later that he thought Maharajji would come back later that night. Maharajji returned forty days later. He had such devotion to the will of

Maharajji that he continued the practice Maharajji had given him for the entire time.

Later, Maharajji commissioned Coloni Walla Baba to paint Kainchi Ashram. In Hindi, Coloni Walla means "one who paints." This is a very loose retelling of a story I heard in Vrindavan years ago. Coloni Walla began work on painting the ashram blue. Maharajji went away. After some time the painting was completed and Maharajji returned. He harshly upbraided Coloni Walla and said that he had ruined the ashram. Maharajji called him names such as fool and idiot, and then told Coloni Walla to repaint the ashram with a different color. So Coloni Walla repainted the entire ashram green. Maharajji returned and again harshly criticized Coloni Walla, called him many names, told him he had ruined the ashram, and told him to repaint the ashram with a different color. Maharajji then went away. Coloni Walla then painted the ashram pink. Upon His return, He summoned Coloni Walla and again reproached him for wrecking the ashram and demanded that Coloni Walla repaint the entire ashram yet again. Maharajji again went away. This time Coloni Walla painted the ashram yellow and orange. When Maharajji returned He said, "Very good." I cannot be sure of the colors or the sequence they were painted, but the story illustrates the love of Maharajji for Coloni Walla because in this way Maharajji was able to give Coloni Walla and his family employment and a place to live for a long time at Kainchi Ashram.

राम राम राम राम राम राम राम राम राम राम राम राम

Listening to Maharajji

There are so many cases where devotees didn't listen to Maharajji, nor do what Maharajji told them to do. A prime example is the Lila of the water supply at Maharajji's Vrindavan Ashram. From the very beginning of the ashram, there was a faithful spring that yielded abundant water. This spring provided so much water that the ashram wall had a small room with a window built in the front facing Parikrama Marg for dispensing water to pilgrims who were doing the propitious circumambulation of Vrindavan. Maharajji told the devotees to never attempt to drill a well there or the water would stop. After Maharajji left His body, they attempted to drill a well, and of course the water stopped. Now the ashram must use tanker trailers to bring in water that is kept in large tanks beneath the ashram. Is this the fault of someone? No, not really. Everything is the Lila of Maharajji.

Maharajji told a young Western woman, who was with Him in the 70s, to go to America and go to school and get her degree. He told her not to get married and instead focus on her studies. She did the exact opposite. She married and had three children. Subsequently she divorced. Twenty years later she returned to India with a devotee friend who had also been with Maharajji in the 70s. While there she remembered what Maharajji told her. When she returned to America, she went to university for a number of years and received her PhD. And she became a respected scholar and university professor. The manager of one of Maharajji's ashrams laughingly told me that this young woman had been "absolutely useless" when she first came to Maharajji, but that through His power, Maharajji was able to make her into a capable, responsible, respected member of society.

राम राम राम राम राम राम राम राम राम राम राम राम

You Are Playing a Role in a Theater

There is no success or failure. There is only "role." It is only a theater. Yes, it seems real, but this life is only real while we are riding in the body. There is simply no one single birth followed by death and then an eternal afterlife in a heaven or a hell. That's not real, at all. HWL Poonja[41] said that death is like sleep. That you close your eyes and the world goes away, then open your eyes and the world returns.

Just as we go to the movies and if it is a good enough movie we are pulled in, forgetting "real life" within the consciousness of the movie. So too, we are pulled into the movie of our individual life and find it almost impossible to remember anything else. It's fine. It's the way it is supposed to be.

You only have a limited time to act out your success or your failure – a limited time to have your pain or your pleasure – on the physical plane. We have got bodies that will last long enough to allow for a full course of that. Lifespans are indeed getting longer, however. Human bodies could indeed begin to last for more than one hundred years or even two hundred years by adjusting things like alkalinity of the blood through natural means. It is all part of evolution. The life expectancy, in America, at the time of the American Revolution (1775-1783) was about 42 years for men and a bit longer for women. Infant mortality rates were high. Now it is different. This is, of course, part of the population explosion but this is how it is supposed to be.

राम राम राम राम राम राम राम राम राम राम राम राम

The 60s

Maharajji is an infinite consciousness who manifested for us in the West in the 1960s and early 1970s. In India, He was active behind the scenes for many years earlier. Indeed, Neem Karoli Baba's Lila probably began quite early in the 20th century, although some stories go back to the latter part of 19th century. Yet it was when He introduced Himself to us in the West that Maharajji truly began the process of becoming part of the global consciousness.

It was very proper that Maharajji's message would be put before so many people during the late 60s, for that was the time of the greatest mass spiritual awakening the world has known. This means that unlike so many other decades, the 60s is not simply a "style," it changed the conscious spiritual and mental makeup of the mass of people. The political movement of the people was indeed suppressed, but the spiritual movement was not suppressed. It kept going. Buddhism, with the same message of love and peace as the teachings of Christ became very popular for both Christians and Jews who were with Maharajji, for example.

Thus the superficial mundane aspects of the 60s were not the most important aspect carried forward from the mass movements of the people. And I believe that a large degree of this deep spiritual growth within people is attributable to Maharajji. And it never manifested in any way that could be pinpointed or quantified by any mass media, including the Web in later days. It was something that happened to individuals in very specific and individual ways. It indeed changed everything beneath the surface and almost everyone of the next generation took a giant super forward step because of it. The mass consciousness expanded and the outer world changed forever. The people literally began morphing into the people of the future. The 6os generation was not like our grandparents just as the grandkids of the 6os generation were handed a greatly changed world. This is not central to America, but is a truly global change that affects all the people of Earth. Maharajji had a big hand in this subtle process.

As far as media is concerned, He let us get a glimpse of Him in "Modern Times" for some years and then escaped. There were very few cameras, almost no audio or video recorders. All we have of Him are at most about 2,000 photographs, about 18 minutes of video with no sound, 3+ hours of audio recording, and several thousand stories about Him as told by others. He has not left, but He is no longer showing Himself to us in the way He once did. Rabboo Joshi told me that Maharajji will give you anything you want, marriage, good job, children, even sex-drugs-rock & roll..., but if you simply take those things, you will miss the real gift. That gift is Maharajji Himself.

राम राम राम राम राम राम राम राम राम राम राम राम

To Awaken You

Sometimes Maharajji will make things utterly difficult for you. It is only in hindsight that you can see why Maharajji did this. When the Chinese invaded India in 1962, devotees asked Maharajji why the Chinese had come. Maharajji said, "To awaken you." I believe that Maharajji makes things difficult because He wants you to awaken to something much better for you.

I lived for many years in a city in the Rockies and did quite well there for twenty years. Although there were some rough times, it seemed that Maharajji was always taking good care of me. Yet underneath I was unhappy because I was not married and the woman that I had dreamed of for very many years could not be found. After discovering Hanuman in Taos, for many years I had planned that someday I would move there so I could practice and serve at His ashram. But I was earning a bunch of money, had a nice home and things were so settled where I was living that I couldn't ever seem to get going. Then, during a period of a year everything seemed to turn against me. I found myself in difficult conflicts with several people, I lost my good job, I lost interest in my home, and things that once seemed fun now seemed shallow. Even tiny things seemed to go against me – things broke, nasty messages were left on my answering machine, and a feeling of negativity came over me. Out of the blue, I'd get reminders of Taos in strange ways like seeing a sign or a bumper sticker, or overhearing people near me talking about Taos. And occasionally people would say things like, "Oh, you should go to Taos to relax." Finally, I began moving my things to Taos. Within two days of arriving in Taos, I met a woman at Maharajji's ashram. We were married in the sunroom at the

Hanuman Temple and we became inseparable for twenty years. I knew deep in my heart and mind for many years that I would meet a very special woman and that we would live in the dharma and travel the world together and serve Maharajji and His satsang and be happy together.

Maharajji made it very rough on me so that I was goaded into making a move that turned out utterly wonderfully. I was able to devote my life to studying and serving Maharajji and my wife and I followed the path of the Lila of Maharajji for many years. My wife has left her body to be with Maharajji now, but I continue the path with Maharajji all the while marveling at the world of love that Maharajji's grace continually creates around me.

राम राम राम राम राम राम राम राम राम राम राम राम

Maharajji Can Speak Through You

Maharajji would make people say things they didn't mean to say, hadn't thought, and might even disagree with their thinking. How strange is that? Gurudat Sharma told me that he was walking across the back compound in Vrindaban. Maharajji was sitting with another man. The man asked Maharajji how long He'd known Gurudat. Maharajji said "Lifetimes." The man said, "No. How can that be?" Maharajji called Gurudat over and asked him, "How long have we know each other?" Gurudat replied

"Lifetimes." although he didn't actually intend to say that.

Many devotees say that they feel Maharajji occasionally speaks through them to make a point with a devotee. There are many instances after Maharajji left His body where this is the case. It has happened to me and to many others I have spoken with on this topic. It may have happened to you. This can include use of healing powers and other powers. Maharajji uses us in many ways as long as you have gotten your "self" out of the way. But if your self is not "out of the way" and you are presuming to direct or instruct people claiming that Maharajji is saying it, you will ultimately get burned. Still, it is all Maharajji's Lila. Don't think that allegedly "channeling" is a good way to develop some followers for yourself, don't bother.

राम राम राम राम राम राम राम राम राम राम राम राम

It has been said that Maharajji also gives temporary powers to devotees in certain circumstances. This can be for healing or instruction or to do some apparently impossible thing. What I experienced in the following has likely happened to other devotees as well. I was performing music in a venue in Tacoma. It was a big event with many performers and being broadcast on the local radio. We all had a very high night. After the gig was done and the house lights were on and the audience had mostly left, I was having some food at one of the quiet tables. Most of the musicians had gone over to the late night music club across the street. I was alone because I sent my wife along with the group saying I would join shortly. One of the waitresses sat with me. As we talked she told me how stressed out she was because of a dire ailment her young son had. If I recall, it was extreme asthma or some condition like that. She was very stressed out about this because she had to constantly deal with it and was very fearful that he would soon die. I reassured her and said that everything was going to be all right, that I felt he would get better very soon. A few months later, I returned there to perform another concert. The waitress rushed up to Radha and me as we walked in and said to me, "You cured my son. When I went home he did not have the disease. He has not had it since then. You saved him." We just blushed. Radha and I just looked at each other and knew that it could only have been Maharajji because I certainly have no ability to do that. Radha said, "No no. God did it." That story was one we did not want told to others. It seemed that Maharajji wanted the boy to be cured and He used this Lila to make it happen.

राम राम राम राम राम राम राम राम राम राम राम राम

The great logician, Kurt Gödel, argued that mathematical concepts and ideas "form an objective reality of their own, which we cannot create or change, but only perceive and describe."[42]

Hinduism is like that. The ancient Hindu *yogis* in the caves through inner sight sought to perceive and describe the underlying nature of the entire physical world, and that the physical world is created by much that is unseen. When we speak of the science of Maharajji, this is what we are talking about. The understanding of it is rather unknowable for all but a very few people. The Hindu seers and sages have looked that deeply within to find the answers to creation that the scientists are looking for outwardly. The further they travel in opposite directions, the closer they come to the same concept of reality.

It all comes down to the You that is "riding in" this body of yours. Everything is about the quality of the movie of your own life and who is actually watching that movie. It is a paradox at one level and completely clear and logical at another level.

राम राम राम राम राम राम राम राम राम राम राम राम

Touching of the Feet

There are so many stories of people rubbing Maharajji's feet. One of the most famous is that of a wanted *dacoit* (bandit) who was at the *tucket* rubbing Maharajji's foot. Rubbing Maharajji's other foot was the head of the state police. Both were utterly transfixed on Maharajji. Maharajji asked the police chief if he knew the man rubbing His other foot. The police chief replied, "No, Maharajji. All I see is you." This illustrates the magnetic power of Maharajji's lotus feet.[43]

Socially, touching of the feet of elders and respected persons, is almost as commonplace as the shaking of hands in the West. For convenience, this is often done as a gesture of reaching down as far as the knees. Gurudat Sharmaji told me that, "The person whose feet are being touched is not the one receiving the benefit of the foot touching. The person who is doing the touching receives all the benefit."[44] I infer from that conversation that the person whose feet are being touched has more *shakti*, *bhakti*, or worldly power than the one touching the feet. It is much like the person whose feet are being touched is literally brimming over with energy, and this in turn is allowing the person touching the feet to "drink" from this pool of spiritual or personal power. In the West, touching of the feet in this manner is completely unthinkable.

Regarding touching of the feet iloveindia.com suggests, "In Indian culture, there are specific occasions when a person is expected to touch his/ her elders' feet. These occasions include before one is departing for or arriving back from a journey, weddings, religious and festive occasions, etc. In earlier times, it was like a custom in India for youngsters to touch their parents' feet first thing in the morning and before going to bed. Though there are many who still follow this rule, the truth is that the tradition is now slowly waning away with time. When an elder person's feet are being touched, he/she, in turn, is supposed to touch the head of the person doing the act and bless him/her for long life, fortune and prosperity. Interestingly, the act of touching feet gets somewhat intensified during certain occasions. For instance, many people prefer prostrating before the deities in temples or before persons of high rank spiritually and even politically. Touching the feet is an integral part of the Indian culture and tradition and not adhering to it by natives is considered as disrespectful."[45]

Dada relates this, "The head of the Goraknath sect came to Kainchi one morning. The Goraknaths are a very great sect of sadhus in India and its head was a very powerful and influential man. He came and sat in Babaji's room. Babaji said to me, 'Dada, Mahant Digvijaynath is a great saint, touch his feet.' I did that. When some other people came, he also told them to touch Mahant Digvijaynath's feet. The third time Babaji said this, Mahant Digvijaynath stood up and said, 'Baba, you who are the saint of saints is sitting before me, and you are making others touch my feet?'"[46]

राम राम राम राम राम राम राम राम राम राम राम राम

A Different Form of Misdirection

When I used to live in Maharajji's Vrindavan Ashram for long periods, I heard many stories not found in the books. Many are contained in this book. One story that seems to illustrate what was really happening constantly around Maharajji describes a day when Maharajji left in a car with four men. After some time (possibly several days?), they returned to the ashram. After Maharajji retired to his room, the men were hanging out together talking about the experience. They were shocked to discover that they had all gone to different places. How is that even slightly possible? It seems that one could never be sure what was really happening when you were around Maharajji. However, this extended to other parts of one's life when you weren't even sitting directly in or near the physical presence of Maharajji.

The word "misdirection" is used to describe something used by magicians doing sleight-of-hand magic (In Hindi, *Jadu*). Maharajji wasn't doing magic, but He seems to have used a different form of misdirection. Multiple things seem to have been happening at the same time around Maharajji. Each person was having his or her own experience. It was perhaps that in Maharajji's presence each was hallucinating. Often when devotees were sitting with Maharajji, He would be saying something apparently to one person, but the depth of the meaning of Maharajji's words was totally aimed at a different devotee. Everything Maharajji did seems to have been some sort of teaching for someone there.

One Western woman described to me that when she was with Maharajji, it often appeared to the other young Westerner kids there that Maharajji treated her very badly. Maharajji would pull her hair and slap her face, and yell at her. Once she saw Maharajji walking with some men on the Parikrama Marg in Vrindavan. She ran to Maharajji and pranamed before Him. Maharajji just stepped right over her and continued walking. As He stepped over her He kicked her in the head. The other young Westerners would ask her how she could possibly stay with Maharajji when He was treating her so badly. But she was not having that sort of experience at all. Everything she experienced coming from Maharajji was with utter love and caring for her. Maharajji was blasting her with a feeling of profound love. She continues to have this experience till the present time, many years later. It is so amazing that with Maharajji nothing appears as you think it is.

राम राम राम राम राम राम राम राम राम राम राम राम

Impossible Experiences for Devotees

Maharajji caused experiences for the devotees that seemed to simply not be possible. Many times these were tiny subtle things. Gurudat Sharma narrated, "Maharajji did not do miracles for show. He did miracles always as a matter of course. Maharajji was traveling with four men. They were going to a house where they expected perhaps three people to be waiting. Two of the men bought eight oranges which they carried to the home. When they all got there, it was discovered that twelve persons were waiting at the house. When the oranges were distributed, everyone received an orange. Only the two men who bought the oranges knew of Maharajji's miracle and He would not let them say anything."[47]

Bhagavan Das stated, "Maharajji performed a miracle a minute. Food, money, a trip to the hospital - whatever the people needed was taken care of... Maharajji had his miracle attainment - that was his illusion. But the miracles were so common that it got to the point where I hardly paid attention to them anymore. It was so matter-of-fact. They were the background of reality. Whenever questioned about them, he would answer, 'I did nothing. God did it.'"[48]

Everything Maharajji did seems to be a "teaching." Riding in a horse cart with Maharajji a man asked Maharajji how the mind could be stilled. At that moment a small child ran out in front of the cart and the driver yanked hard on the reins to stop the horse. Maharajji said, "Like that."

After studying Maharajji for more than 30 years, I feel that Maharajji had some sort of "force field" around him that was constantly creating these anomalies. I don't feel that Maharajji was using any sort of thinking-power such as a normal thinking person might do. Maharajji arrived and things changed. It was almost like the laws of physics changed around Him. Maharajji is/was always in control, however. Maharajji was at the center of this.

Maharajji talked to animals and they understood what He was saying. The out-of-control horse could be quickly calmed when Maharajji talked to it. A devotee even saw Maharajji secretly speaking to the Hanuman murti the day before His Lila of the murti falling unscathed to the floor below.

राम राम राम राम राम राम राम राम राम राम राम राम

So many times it was reported that Maharajji just "wasn't there." His body was there, but He had temporarily left it to go to some other place – perhaps using His light-body or by traveling on the astral plane. Saraswati mentioned that she was in the car with Maharajji once, when Maharajji's body became small, shrunken, and rather gray. Maharajji had "checked out" to go someplace else for some reason. He just wasn't there. After some time, He returned to His body and He again appeared as normal.

Maharajji showed us all different things. For example, in 2010, one Canadian woman (a really dear friend) said that she was always told not to tell stories of Maharajji or speak about Him to people. My late wife, Radha Rani, refused to speak about her beliefs in Maharajji to others outside of satsang, and then only rarely within satsang. I have heard this same thing from others. After reflecting on this, I realized that I had been told the opposite – that I should speak about Maharajji very much and should give information about Maharajji and Maharajji related materials to everyone in the world.

राम राम राम राम राम राम राम राम राम राम राम राम

When all the young Westerners came to India to meet Maharajji, He did not require that they study Hinduism. Yes, many did, because that was their own positive spiritual path. And indeed, what is left in Maharajji's ashrams in India is a very Hindu scene with very Hindu practices. Practice is one of the ways to freeing the mind and extricating yourself from the drama of your own life so that you can begin a deeper contemplation of Maharajji. Singing of *kirtan*[49], performing aarti, meditation, seva (selfless service), yoga are all helpful in freeing you. Many of Maharajji's Western devotees adopted Buddhist practices. Perhaps we could say they became Buddhists. This also seems quite natural.

Love everyone (everything), Feed (serve) everyone, Remember God (in everything), Give up attachment, and Tell the Truth. These can be said to be the essential teaching from Maharajji. The most basic practice required is to "remember" Maharajji. A loving remembrance of Maharajji brings Him closer. Maharajji said, "Whoever remembers me. I go to them." Remembering Maharajji is for your benefit because Maharajji does not forget even His most forgetful persons.

As an illustration of a "small" teaching directly spoken by Maharajji, He told Gurudat: "Even if you have *lakhs* (hundreds of thousands) of people as supporters, as followers, and as attendants always at your command, you must personally attend to: *khati** (kay-tee) - cultivation, *pati** (pa-tee) - writing letters, *binti** (bin-tee)(or vin-tee) - worship, *ghorey katang** - The tying of the saddle on the back of the horse." (*indicates Sanskrit)

राम राम राम राम राम राम राम राम राम राम राम राम

Maharajji would do His "miracles" and people would look to Him like He'd done it. But Maharajji said, "I don't do anything. God does it all." Perhaps the reason that we focus on Maharajji is because of His power - the power to help our individual lives. Or maybe, Maharajji's satsang clings to Him because He is our father and we know He manifests a power that cannot die.

राम राम राम राम राम राम राम राम राम राम राम राम

Sometimes I feel almost "driven" by Maharajji. When I want to sit and do nothing he creates these situations where I have to do many things. Strange circumstances. Then I get all worried about how I can possibly do these things. Almost always when I begin moving on the thing, the doors open, the way is paved, the people are waiting all along the path to help and guide me. He always has an answer. It is not my Jivatma that is worried. It is my body, my mind (brain). It is a constant battle. Well, not a battle actually, but a constant tension between the brain and a different reality. I know that Maharajji will take care of it, and He always does. My Jivatma within me is just quietly residing in there and is always OK. Maharajji always reminds me of that. Since I realized that Maharajji (some thirty years ago) is doing these things in my life, I have grown to rely on this more and more.

राम राम राम राम राम राम राम राम राम राम राम राम

Gurudatji told that "Maharajji was living in a forest in Bihar. There was a report among the local people that Maharajji had a lot of guns and ammunition there. When the police went there to investigate, they found only big bundles of sticks."[50] What could have been about? This is the only story that I know of that specifically says that Maharajji was in Bihar.

राम राम राम राम राम राम राम राम राम राम राम राम

When it came time to make murtis of Maharajji there was a big problem because no one knew if Maharajji was short or tall, if he was fat or thin. Devotees experienced Him in so many forms. Even in the photographs, Maharajji sometimes looked so different.

Maharajji is like the candle flame, never appearing the same for more than a moment.

राम राम राम राम राम राम राम राम राम राम राम राम

Maharajji Is a Manifestation

Your karma must play out for you in this life. But there are many views as to what karma is and its interaction with reincarnation (transmigration of souls). Maharajji seems to go beyond karma, yet it was Ram Dass that implied that even Maharajji had karma in that he married, as was expected of Him, and had three children. But to view that mundane side of the Maharajji equation diverts from the real focus on "who" Maharajji is. I don't believe for one moment that Maharajji's marriage is karma. I believe it is yet another Lila of Maharajji.

Maharajji is not an incarnation. Maharajji is a manifestation, much the way Krishna tells Arjuna, in the "Bhagavad Gita," that He is a manifestation. Although we can point to an apparent birth, I believe

Maharajji did not take a birth on earth and then develop powers. I believe He brings it all with Him, when He manifests as an apparent body to be more or less in physical form, so He can interact directly with us. How this could be done is a major mystery to us. It is all His Lila.

राम राम राम राम राम राम राम राम राम राम राम राम

There are so many great people in so many great lineages. Ramana Maharshi, Swami Ramakrishna, Shirdi Sai Baba, and more, both known and unknown, by the masses. These are divine people. Maharajji is not a person and never was. He appeared to be a person, but He was not.

राम राम राम राम राम राम राम राम राम राम राम राम

People everywhere are now going about their daily lives. Everyone everywhere is seeking and searching. What are they searching for? Pleasure? Gratification? Satiation? Are we only driven by chemicals coursing through our bodies and by psychological embeds? I believe that everyone is searching for Maharajji in one way or another. Everyone is searching for the one who loves them unconditionally and who cares about them and who knows all about them. Whether seen or unseen, this is Maharajji. To know that Maharajji exists is its own grace. Just to hear the name Neem Karoli Baba in its many forms is grace. If you (your Jivatma) are not ready, you will not recognize this name or His photo. But if you are ready…, ahhhhh.

People don't usually go to the doctor unless they are sick. Maharajji is the Maha-doctor. Maharajji is the cure for so many things for so many people; whatever the sickness. This doesn't mean disease, necessarily. People can be sick and tired of living in a loveless closed-hearted world, or sick of a family that is abusive or doesn't understand them, or sick of working on the treadmill of a thankless heartless corporation. Many persons have become devotees of Maharajji because of heavy-duty health issues. Maharajji helps their heart to accept their situation and to find the guidance they are seeking. If one who comes to Maharajji is open and innocent and loving, Maharajji pulls them right in. If someone comes with an agenda of their own, He sends them away. Maharajji knows you and He knows what is in your heart.

राम राम राम राम राम राम राम राम राम राम राम राम

Love Is a Force

The scientists don't actually see Love as a force. Maharajji is that force of Love. It is because of Love that He was here for us and continues to be here for us. Taxing our minds is not the answer. We, as normal humans, cannot think it through. It simply exhausts us and can indeed make us crazy. What is happening is not knowable. The Greater Consciousness (Atma) is not focused on the physical plane. It creates the physical plane. What Maharajji is working with is a greater love, a greater "science" that is also outside the physical plane. And Maharajji manifested things here on the physical plane.

Yet it is Love that is everything that builds all of life on the physical plane. It is the only thing worth exploring. For humans it has so many meanings and interpretations. Even on a battlefield there is so much love going on. Within the battle, is the intense love that the soldiers feel for each other at the core of the fight. They will often risk their own death to save the lives of the others, their brothers in arms. No matter how they "act," no matter how they have fear, no matter how much they "hate" the enemy, no matter how the army's organization may behave, they carry out this intense action within a strange cocoon of love. They are at the very edge of life and death. If one dies, he goes directly into the utter Love outside the physical plane.

राम राम राम राम राम राम राम राम राम राम राम राम

Maharajji, the fully realized being appearing in physical form, knows that the core is Love, so when we meet Maharajji, we are "in love." Within love is everything wondrous and marvelous. Love is the core of everything. Love is the manifestation of the divine. Love is an essential part of the procreation process.

During the procreation process we are so close to the door of birth that we can feel such intense Love, just as near the door of death of bodies we so often feel an overpowering Love, overpowering pleasure of love. It must also be said that the animal nature can take over during sex and create a loveless intercourse that is not what is meant here. The times when we feel the most love in our lives is when we are closest to our Jivatmas. We are closer to the core, which is Love. Maharajji is called "The Miracle of Love" because throughout all the Lilas, He manifested Love. Regardless of how His dance was perceived, the core is/ was love.

Maharajji's Love is not narrow love. Not the "I love you" love from the movies. It is the Really Big Love. The omnipotent love for all. It's like love for your spouse, your children, your friend, a possession, but also for every animal, every plant, for the molecules in all of us and in everything..., for every foe or enemy or antagonist, including germs, viruses and diseases. This includes every blade of grass, every stone in the path, every nail in the rickshaw, every button on the blouse, every fiber in the blanket. This means an absolute absence of hate. Jesus taught this to all. You must love all. Even The Beatles taught this when they sang, "All You Need is Love." That mantra should remain in everyone's mind. For this to work for you, you must see (feel) the greater love for everything that is and was and ever will be. In essence, you must "Be Love."

राम राम राम राम राम राम राम राम राम राम राम राम

Maharajji said, "Even if a person hurts you, give him love. The worst punishment is to throw someone out of your heart... You should love everyone as God, and love each other."

Maharajji said, "If you cannot love each other, you cannot achieve your goal."

Maharajji said, "Love is the strongest medicine. It is more powerful than electricity."

राम राम राम राम राम राम राम राम राम राम राम राम

It all abides in Love and it is All One (*Sub ek*). Love is the carrier current in the All One. There is only one thing happening and it is happening within a stream of love. The "you" that you think is a human and the entire Earth are not separate things. The earth lives and breathes as you do. It is a living entity. Of the life forms on Earth only about 3% are animals while 97% are plants. This is staggering. Who are humans? What do we think we are doing here? What do we see our places as being? Clearly the understanding of what reality is can use an upgrade. Maharajji has helped so many expand their concept of reality and "see the big picture." Not all of us, but the ones who are ready.

Maharajji said, "The best form to worship God is every form." Many people are being helped by God every day. God is their constant companion. They believe in God. They worship God. They pray to God. They thank God. God protects them. God goes with them. God helps them. God blesses them. The universal God consciousness is Atma. You can see God in a flower.

राम राम राम राम राम राम राम राम राम राम राम राम

Circle of Beliefs

The people around Maharajji, in what is called "the satsang," form a complete circle of beliefs around Him. One couple that spent a lot of time with Maharajji in the 70s told me, "Neem Karoli Baba was a really nice guy, but this talk of him being God is completely not true." To hear people say this, by the way, is extremely rare. Yet, I still believe that it is another Lila of Maharajji that He would ensure there were people to say such things so that you always have an apparent "way out."

Others, on the other opposite side of that circle around Maharajji, say that Maharajji is Guru of Gurus, Lord of Lords, God of Gods, The Lord God. All around the circle, Maharajji has people who view Him from their own perspective that has come from their own backgrounds and temperaments. Those brought up as Christians seem to see Him as an incarnation of Jesus, for example. Maybe atheists see Maharajji as a magician. I don't know. But Maharajji is not just a guy in the center of this circle. This is all the Lila of Maharajji. He IS the circle. It is ALL His play, His Lila. You don't even get to know that Maharajji exists unless you are sufficiently evolved to know.

Maharajji was very enamored with Jesus and spoke of him often, I am told. Tears would come to Maharajji's eyes as He spoke of Jesus. Some devotees got the feeling that Maharajji knew Jesus personally. Before I read the "Jesus Lived in India" book, I wasn't so impressed with Jesus because of the bloodthirsty nature of the church institutions founded in Jesus' name, but afterwards I realized that Jesus was the coolest of all the devotees. Since then, I have had a very strong desire to visit Jesus' grave in Kashmir and to find the temple/church at the place where Mary, Jesus' mother, is alleged to have left her body on the journey back to India with her son.

I don't think Maharajji was an incarnation of Jesus, as some have suggested. Since reading "Jesus Lived in India"[51], I have such a strong hit that Jesus went to Maharajji all those years ago and hung out at Maharajji's tucket, like all the devotees did, basking in the bliss of being in the presence of Maharajji. Then like most of Maharajji's devotees, Jesus went off to change the world. When he referred to "my father who is in Heaven," he was referring to Maharajji in India. That, of course, flies totally in the face of the established doctrines of the churches.

राम राम राम राम राम राम राम राम राम राम राम राम

Devotees - Satsang

I have met some of the most amazing devotees in Maharajji's satsang. The people who were directly with Maharajji and took Maharajji's darshan are generally indescribable. There is a quality about them that is very "real." There is a sense of calmness about them. They have widely differing personalities and walks of life. Yet their love for Maharajji is immense. The Western kids who were with Maharajji in the '70s are much older now, and they continue to carry Maharajji so lovingly in their hearts and minds.

Satsang is like Maharajji's secret society. Once He has drawn you in, you never want to get out from beneath His blanket. Even if you do not go to His temples or associate with His satsang, He is with you. When you remember Him, He comes to you. When you do not remember Him, He just watches and does what He wants. He is not a He, by the way. We just refer to Maharajji in the form of Neem Karoli Baba as He. There is something more than gender identification going on.

राम राम राम राम राम राम राम राम राम राम राम राम

Shivaya Baba once said to me, "You might as well get along with the people in the satsang because you're going to know them for the rest of your life."

राम राम राम राम राम राम राम राम राम राम राम राम

Although these early devotees are very connected to each other in a very family-like way, Maharajji's satsang is not a social scene. We in satsang are joined by the experience of our journey on the spiritual path just as much as the young people of the '60s and '70s were when they met Maharajji. We are joined by our practice and our sense of Maharajji and our communication with Him.

Naturally, life can be called somewhat strange for Maharajji's satsang. They rely on Maharajji for everything. For non-satsang people this is incomprehensible in so many ways. Devotees often wait for Maharajji to provide the solution, the next step, or to make right a situation that appears wrong. In a way, it is the ultimate "Let Go and Let God" attitude. Waiting for your Guru to tell you what to do is pretty scary for non-satsang. It's pretty scary for devotees too, at first. But it always works out.

It is not necessary for you to know other devotees of Maharajji, but it helps your heart to be with them. Many people are seeking to be in community with other people who worship Maharajji, who love Maharajji, who do puja to Maharajji and to Hanuman. This is difficult, but not impossible. In America there is the Taos Hanuman Temple[52] in New Mexico, and there is the Kashi Ashram[53] in Florida. There are devotees of Neem Karoli Baba at these places. You can visit Ram Dass on Maui Hawaii, however, special arrangements are required. You can attend a Krishna Das kirtan gathering in New York or anywhere else he is leading kirtan. Jai Uttal holds marvelous kirtan gatherings in many locations. The truth is that it is up to Maharajji (and your karma) to provide you with satsang friends. He will, if you really want it and you make the effort – sometimes a lot of effort. Continue to do your personal practice. If you are ready to be pulled closer to satsang, Maharajji will do it. Being in satsang is easy and it is difficult. Be open to Maharajji's Lila. It is loving and also your desire for satsang is burning up uncooked seeds.

राम राम राम राम राम राम राम राम राम राम राम राम

Maharajji said, "We meet only those people with whom our meeting is predestined. Duration of association with each person is also preordained. One should not grieve if one is separated or if the association does not last long."

राम राम राम राम राम राम राम राम राम राम राम राम

That Maharajji allowed us to see Him, hear Him, have His darshan, is a precursor to the new world that lies ahead and a major boon to His devotees. His appearance, fleeting though it may have been, is the beginning. His influence on many key people has changed many things.

You aren't meeting Maharajji in a physical form. Even the people who were with Maharajji when He was in the manifested physical form of Neem Karoli Baba weren't meeting Him that way. You are meeting Maharajji on another plane (a higher level) of consciousness. That is where Maharajji has got hold of you. It is not required that you do anything to be a member. In fact, it is the opposite. You notice the Lilas and wonder what is happening. Then one day you realize that you have entered the Lila of Maharajji.

You might think that strange things, inexplicable things, are happening to you. And they become overpowering sometimes. It may take years to discover that Maharajji is behind it. This is why Maharajji's satsang do not proselytize. No one will try to get you to join anything. All you can do is look for the answer to the questions this brings about, and these answers will be provided by Maharajji as you require them.

राम राम राम राम राम राम राम राम राम राम राम राम

It's a feeling of life change, in a way. You might say, "How did my life get to be so weird?" Maybe it was the photograph of Maharajji that you looked at. That photograph also saw you. Maharajji looked into your heart and saw that you were ready to know about the next steps. Maybe Maharajji visited you one day, or talked with you on the street, or anywhere really. Maybe in your anguish about something, your inner consciousness called to a greater consciousness.

If you are called to Maharajji, Maharajji most likely got ahold of you long before you realized it, even in another life. Yet Maharajji does not pull you to know Him consciously until you (with the help of your own Jivatma) are ready. How can it be otherwise? Only a small number of people are even ready to know about Maharajji. If you aren't ready, you can see references to

Maharajji, or even drive by His ashrams many times without Maharajji pulling you in.

After you become conscious of Maharajji, conscious that a greater pure force of love and goodness has you, you wonder what others could possible be thinking, or how they get through their days or how they perceive what they are doing in this life.

राम राम राम राम राम राम राम राम राम राम राम राम

Maharajji does not always make life easier for His devotees. Actually, He sometimes makes things quite difficult. He challenges the mind of His devotees to again surrender to their hearts, to their Jivatma souls, indeed, to Him.

Maharajji will "put you through it." That is the only way to say it. Maharajji is teaching all His devotees. He is teaching you every day. The lessons are often very difficult. The juxtapositions of events are often so different. It has been said that Maharajji will put you in a difficult position or put you totally in the wrong, and then pull you out of it and put you in the reverse position. It seems that "reversal" is a big part of Maharajji's Lila. In this manner of reversals, Maharajji stretches you ever further in realizing aspects of life in all directions.

Maharajji may solve the problem for you, but Maharajji probably caused the problem for you in the first place. It's just a question of who you think the "you" is that has the problem. Once you surrender to the Lila, there are no options. Maharajji, as your Guru, creates all situations. And all the people who appear to you at any given moment, are Maharajji. To realize Maharajji being your brother Bob, your boss, or lover, or teammate is a great boon. All you can do is love that person as you love your Guru, as you love Maharajji. To do that changes everything. Because inside of every one of them, they are as much Maharajji as you are.

Maharajji said, "Don't be afraid of misfortune. Dogs bark but the elephant walks on, he does not care."

राम राम राम राम राम राम राम राम राम राम राम राम

As Ravi Das wrote, "It was not a matter of him being out of his body, he was definitely in his body in the sixties under that plaid blanket wiggling his finger and the world responding. Maharaji was doing his thing in many weird places in Uttar Pradesh since the 1930's. So it's OK to use me Babaji, it's an honor. Some people in the Indian way of thinking imagine Maharaji is God-incarnate, like an Avatar, like Ram, the incarnation of Hanuman. A guru they believe takes control of the switch long before you are reborn. He can break karmic cycles, that's why it is foolish to pooh-pooh gurus. I would give up billions of dollars if offered as a trade to never having met Maharaji. I'm addicted but it's not all pleasure..."[54]

राम राम राम राम राम राम राम राम राम राम राम राम

Maharajji's devotees could be described as "disciples." Maharajji carefully selects these devotees, often apparently selecting them from out of the masses to bestow His grace on them in so many ways. It is as if Maharajji drew in devotees to His merry band of people, who do the work of the dharma of Maharajji, to heal the world and to bring us all to a more Godlike understanding of the nature of being human manifestations of God. His devotees use so many small and large means.

It doesn't seem to have been necessary to actually meet Maharajji, in the form of Neem Karoli Baba, to be called into service by Maharajji or to find yourself in His Lila.

Once a devotee has realized Maharajji, nothing will ever be the same.

राम राम राम राम राम राम राम राम राम राम राम राम

Miracles of Saints

Saints have the power to transmute things (i.e. by blessing them). Actually we can all unconsciously do this, or more often, affect things negatively with mental attitudes. Saints can do this positive blessing consciously and with strong intention. As Masaru Emoto's[55] experiments with ice crystals may have indicated, we can and do alter things around us with intention. Who is doing the altering? Is it Jivatma or brainpower? We can't be sure, can we? But it seems to be demonstrable. Imagine the focused power of Maharajji on these things. Mataji too. India has millions of these stories of prayer, practice, and intention.

In Christian theology schools, they simply do not teach that there are supernatural beings roaming the earth, yet there is a belief in saints. This means people who are capable of performing "miracles" to heal the sick, hold back a flood, or do other things that are inexplicable. Where do the saint-like qualities of Maharajji fit into this? If Maharajji had been a Catholic, surely He would have been recognized and canonized by the church, based on so many reports of the miracles He performed in abundance. Because Maharajji remained hidden from the West within the depths of Indian culture, little would have been known about Him outside of India had Maharajji not pulled Ram Dass to Him to learn and later teach in the West. It is Maharajji's grace that we in the West even heard about Him.

There are countless stories in India of the miracles of saints. Many Indian saints have demonstrated such miracles. Maharajji performed every one of those miracles that have been ascribed to many other saints, and more. How can we reconcile the presence of saints on Earth? How is it possible for a person to be able to do these things? Is it possible for there to have been a greater demonstration of saintly powers?

The existence of the stories of the Lilas of Neem Karoli Baba Maharajji is a remarkable insight into this phenomenon. Maharajji cannot be dismissed as a simple trickster. There is ample proof that Maharajji was beyond remarkable. Everything about Maharajji is an indication of an archetype of the new Avatar. He was literally the epitome of complete non-attachment. He performed miracles that have been amply described. He cared for many thousands of people. He fed perhaps millions of people in India in the course of time that we can track Maharajji as Neem Karoli Baba.

Dada Mukherjee describes that, "One day, Babaji asked Shukla to go to the wife of Dan Singh Bisht and ask for her car. Shukla said, 'In order that she will realize that I need the car for you and not for me, I shall have to talk to her about you and say you are here.' Babaji then laughingly replied, 'You are very intelligent, I did not think of this problem, how did you think of it? But what is to be done now? I have to go.' While standing there enjoying his talk, another car arrived. There was no one else in the car and Babaji got into it and drove away. Shukla said no one had known what his problem was nor how it was solved, but he could come and go as was necessary. This was how his work went on."[56]

Asked of satsang in India, "Who is Neem Karoli Baba? Who is Maharajji?" The answer is, "He is God." This being the case, that a manifestation of God (Atma – all knowing fully realized consciousness) has finally been "caught" by us humans, then it seems to follow that God is always on Earth among us in some form, or indeed several forms.

Seva

Seva is a Sanskrit word for selfless service which is performed without any expectation of result or award for the person performing it. The idea of selfless service (seva also sewa) is an important concept in most Indian religions and *yogic* traditions. Because God is perceived as having a relationship with others, as well as oneself, serving other people is considered an essential devotional practice of indirectly serving God. Service to make life easier for others. It is one of central tenets of Sikhism. "Living creatures are nourished by food, and food is nourished by rain; rain itself is the water of life, which comes from selfless worship and service." - Bhagavad Gita, 3.14. Selfless service is also important in Christianity. Jesus often preached it and both Peter and Paul, respectively, wrote about it.[57]

Service (seva) to Maharajji is often service to others and indeed to everyone. Your seva within Maharajji's ashrams is usually simple. There are prescribed guidelines for caretakers, ashram staff and pujaris. Much of the seva with the ashram revolves around food preparation and distribution, as well as attending to the cleanliness and good order of the ashram. This seva must be done without intruding your personal thoughts into the execution of your duties. One would clear their mind to accomplish these seva duties.

Maharajji said, "Work has to be done. What is to be done tomorrow must be done today, and what is to be done today must be done right now."

Devotees of Maharajji perform seva for Him in many ways. Deep devotees literally serve Him with almost every action they take. All actions are performed as selfless service to Maharajji. Within Maharajji's ashrams, seva is performed in food preparation, chai making, food service, dishwashing, cleaning, doing laundry, building construction & maintenance, gardening, caring for elderly and infirmed persons, office work, gathering supplies, and various duties with the temple(s).

Outside of the ashrams, seva is the dedication of all your actions to Maharajji, to the Supreme God consciousness, in whatever form they may take within your job, within your business, within your family, within your community, and in all forms. For Maharajji's devotees, this means that anything and everything you do is dedicated to Maharajji as seva. When seva is performed, one does everything possible to make the result of the seva as perfect and correct as possible, although you cannot be attached to how the results look to you when all is said and done. Performance of seva correctly is for your own benefit as well as those being served. An important attribute is that within your act of seva is an infusion of Love and positive intention. This Love and positive intention benefits the server and the served.

Maharajji said, "Work is worship."

You want to spend your time in seva as a meditation upon Maharajji to help you hear what Maharajji wants you to do. The preparation of food has some specific rules. In American culture this has come to be called, "cooking with intention." Yet intention implies a thought process. With the food preparation of the ashram is a quality of removing yourself and your mind from the equation and thereby being a channel for Maharajji to put whatever intention He wishes into the food. We never taste the food while cooking before it is offered to Maharajji.

राम राम राम राम राम राम राम राम राम राम राम राम

A Sort of Madness

For many devotees, there is a sort of madness or mania associated with the devotion to Maharajji. Devotees are dealing with differences in terms of perceiving one's life that the rational mind refuses to acknowledge or accept. Particularly the minds of other people. Often devotees of Maharajji have families that cannot comprehend what has happened to them. They do not understand that something happened to you and you are following a different path, growing in a different direction. This is not because of ill will toward one's family but because of immense good will on your new path.

Another story Gurudatji told me was this. "A man was having the darshan of Maharajji. Maharajji gave this man a very big case of *puris*[58]. Something like thirty-six puris in that package. The man was trying to refuse so much *prasad* because he was traveling by train and with his other baggage it would be very difficult. Still, Maharajji persisted and the man took the puris. Riding on the train the man felt the train begin to slow a little and at the same time he began to notice an elephant in the distance running toward the train. As the train continued to slow the elephant continued to run at the train. When the train finally stopped the elephant came directly to the window. The man fed all the puris to the elephant."[59]

Tapasya

Devotion to Maharajji is often a '*tapasya*'. Here is a good definition from Wikipedia. "Tapas (tapas, Sanskrit: तपस्) means deep meditation, effort to achieve self-realization, sometimes involving solitude, hermitism or asceticism; it is derived from the word root tap (Sanskrit: तप् or ताप) which depending on context means 'heat' from fire or weather, or blaze, burn, shine, penance, pain, suffering, mortification. In Vedic literature of Hinduism, fusion words based on tapas are widely used to expound several spiritual concepts that develop through heat or inner energy, such as meditation, any process to reach special observations and insights, the spiritual ecstasy of a yogin or tāpasa (a Vriddhi derivative meaning 'a practitioner of austerities, an ascetic'), even warmth of sexual intimacy. In certain contexts, the term is also used to mean penance, suffering, austerity, pious activity, as well as misery. The fusion word tapasvini (Sanskrit: तपस्विनी), for example, means a female devotee or pious woman, 'an ascetic, someone practicing austerities', or in some contexts it can mean poor, miserable woman. In the yogic tradition it is the fire that burns within that is needed for the sanyasi to achieve the very difficult goal of enlightenment, to foster self-control, one mindedness and focus, simplicity, wisdom, integrity. It is used to develop and discipline the body, mind and character; control of mind; and complete eradication of all desires - through discipline of body, correct speech, telling only the truth, correct thought, non violence, correct action, love for all, devotion to god, developing the ability to remain tranquil and balanced in every situation, act without any selfish motive or thought of reward, with an unshakable faith in god."[60]

Maharajji is always in the process of forming you into a purer, happier, more beautiful, more powerful person according to the lines of your karma, your programming, and your destiny in your current life. It does not mean that you devote to Maharajji and then He turns you into a movie star. He may well turn you into a star in some way, but He is just as likely to later take stardom away, and then maybe even restore your stardom in a different way.

Maharajji said, "If you want to see God, kill desires. Desires are in the mind. When you have a desire for something, don't act on it and it will go away. If you desire to drink this cup of tea, don't, and the desire for it will fall away."

All that is about the fire of tapas. And as the fire burns it removes the things that are keeping you out of the mainstream of the love that is the core of existence regardless of the apparent manifestation on the outside. Ram Dass said, "Fame and shame and pleasure and pain are all the same." It's all about the fire of tapas within you.

राम राम राम राम राम राम राम राम राम राम राम राम

Human Desires Don't Matter

Your human desires don't really matter. The brain, often the lower functions of the brain, drives most desires, although many desires are an effect of your karma. The results of your actions don't matter. You cannot be attached to any results. What matters? Loving all, Serving all, Remembering God and Telling the Truth.

The menu of apparent choices that is in your mind is not the same menu that Maharajji sees for your life. Your menu is so limited that it is best to completely discard it through your surrender to Maharajji. You can't say, "OK, Maharajji, 1 surrender. Now please give me a million dollars." It doesn't work that way. Maybe Maharajji will give you a million dollars someday. He certainly is more than capable of giving you millions of dollars. It is more likely that, if you are to receive millions of dollars, Maharajji will put you on a path to a million dollars. You must be ready for something like that so if you are to receive that, then He will prepare you to live dharmically with such a sum of money.

People often wish for things that cannot be granted in this life, and they are fixed on the apparent problem. It is better to simply see God in the movie of your life. The old British slogan, "Keep Calm and Carry On" is a phrase that Radhika spread around in many ways to the satsang and the people of Taos to good effect. These are wise words for all of us. If we feel that we have fully surrendered to Maharajji and then He doesn't give us the things on our own perceived menu, we will get upset and blame Maharajji. How foolish. It is like Maharajji giving you the most wonderful milksweet and you are upset because He did not give you khir[61]. You should tuck into that milksweet and realize the wonderfulness of it without any thought for the khir. Although the khir will surely arrive at another time.

In Rabboo Joshi's wonderful book about Maharajji called "1 and My Father are One," he mentions, "It is like Maharajji put a 'chip' inside you." This is true. So many devotees can relate to this concept. Often this chip has been put there long before you realize who Maharajji is or that He has done this.

If you are going through something difficult, remember that Maharajji has people waiting at every gate for you, to serve you and help you through. Be open to the grace of Maharajji. However, even your openness is not required. Maharajji has more than enough power to infuse any situation with His grace.

राम राम राम राम राम राम राम राम राम राम राम राम

Maharajji Forgives

Maharajji forgives just about anything without the need for your confession. You must be good, yet what you might think of as good could be a bit different than you were taught. Maharajji as a fully realized being can see all of the elements of your being apparently good or not good.

In a way, Being Good is not a "goal." If there were a goal it would be to BE Maharajji. What a wonderful world it would be if we could achieve being Maharajji. What better role model could be found than Maharajji? In the same way, Maharajji's ashrams are a wonderful example to use as a role model for your home. This is not to say that you would make your home a public ashram, but that you would live in your home in the same way you would live within the ashram. All Hindu homes have temples, and indeed are temples. If you think that you are living in an ashram, you certainly approach the day differently.

Finding your own center of calm during so many activities that often appear chaotic is the key. For devotees your home must be your ashram. Your home must have a sacred quality that you bring to bear on the vibration. A small personal temple helps to maintain the sacred quality of your environment. All devotees have "puja tables" (altars) with deities, photos of Maharajji and other holy people such as great saints. This is an essential element in the maintenance of the energy of your house.

राम राम राम राम राम राम राम राम राम राम राम राम

Ram Ram

"Ram Ram Ram Ram Ram Ram" is the mantra Maharajji repeated constantly. It has been reported that at some times Maharajji repeated the mantra "Radha, Radha, Radha, Radha, Radha Radha," saying the name of the Radha Rani, consort of Krishna, incarnation of Hindu goddess Lakshmi who is absolutely adored in the *Brij*[52] area of India.

But generally speaking, it is the name of Ram that Maharajji said constantly and generally silently. One Western devotee who was with Maharajji in the '70s said that the Western kids joked that it looked like Maharajji was chewing gum because His jaw was almost constantly moving as he continued His mantra.

Maharajji often did *Japa*[63] writing Rams (राम राम) on papers and in notebooks. Maharajji gave many of these sheets of paper to devotees.

This is most assuredly the reason for adoption of the salutation of Ram Ram among Maharajji's satsang, as well as prevalent in the local area surrounding Chitrakut. "Radhe Radhe" and "Hare Krishna" are used extensively in the Brij, Mathura, and Vrindavan area, "Om Nama Shivaya" in the mountains, and "Jai Gurudev" among other satsangs such as that of Maharishi Mahesh Yogi. There are many different salutations among the many Hindu sects of India. Maharajji said that by taking the name of Ram, all things are accomplished.

However, the fact that Maharajji repeated Ram Ram as a mantra practice rather than simply using it as a greeting is significant. It seems therefore, that we have something to learn from this. Surely it seems like a very good idea to cultivate the habit of constantly chanting the name of Ram silently and discretely within ourselves.

In the "Mahabharata," Shiva states that uttering "Ram" three times is equal to pronouncing a thousand other names of God. Mahatma Gandhi also often used the Ram mantra. "Ram Ram" was the last thing Mahatma Gandhi said when he was assassinated.

The incomparable Bhagavan Das, offers the following insight, "Once, I borrowed a friend's Land Rover and drove up to see Maharajji in Vrindavan at a small spiritual gathering. It was beautiful, as they usually were. Everyone was happy and fulfilled. Suddenly, Maharajji jumped off his tucket (a low wooden bed) and announced, 'Lets go to Agra!' Everyone leapt up to escort him out. I thought he'd get into one of the other cars and I'd follow behind. He looked over at the Land Rover, hopped in, and slammed the door shut. I got in, and soon we were driving down the trunk road from Vrindavan to Agra. On Indian roads, including the national highway, were cows, rickshaw wallahs, dogs, wild goats, and even chickens on the loose! It was extremely dangerous, and fatal accidents were not uncommon. I was going about forty-five miles per hour, which is pretty fast in India. Maharajji looked over at me and said, 'Jaldi karo! Jaldi Karo! (Go faster! Go faster!)' I inched it up a little. Then Maharajji yelled 'Jali, jali, jaldi karo!' and I went a little faster. He didn't seem satisfied, so I floored it all the way to Agra. As the speed increased, we were going so fast that I could barely hold onto the steering wheel. The jeep lurched recklessly on the bumpy road.

"Then the strangest thing happened. I looked over at Maharajji's seat, and there was nothing but his crumpled blanket. I held onto the wheel with one hand and held up the blanket with the other - and there really was nothing there! I swore to myself that I would never drive that fast again. I thought, 'This can't be happening; this can't be true.' But there was nothing I could do but let go of my ideas of how the moment should be. And by letting go, I broke through. I realized that at any given time, there was only the moment. No more. No less. Only the moment. And then came the rush. My whole body started pulsating with ecstasy. It was an unbelievable experience, like being in two universes at once. The moment was here now, and so was I. I don't know how long it lasted (its an hour and a half to Agra) because I was in eternity. I looked over again and there was Maharajji sitting next to me, wearing his blanket, chewing his Rams. 'Ramramramramramramramramramram!' We pulled up in Agra. Maharajji threw the door open and leapt out of the car just like a monkey. Maharajji was a Ram transmitter. He sounded like a siren. 'Ramramramramramramramramramram!' One of the attainments of great saints is that they become transmitting stations. They go 'on the air.' a cosmic channel. Maharajji was broadcasting blessings every

m o m e n t   o f   t h e   d a y .
'Ramramramramramramramramramram!'"[64]

राम राम राम राम राम राम राम राम राम राम राम राम

A New Archetype

Maharajji's appearance in form at the beginning of
a completely new era of human existence is of supreme
importance. Maharajji acts in a spiritual, non-religious,
fully realized, super-conscious way in all things, yet He
remains a complete renunciate, appearing in the world
but unattached to the world. Maharajji exhibits all the
power of the Gods of old.

However, Maharajji does not bring to bear
powerful armies of soldiers to do battle against the
demons as was done by Lord Krishna and Lord Ram.
Maharajji has unleashed a small army of benign, often
humble "do-gooder" devotees to aid the world, much
as Lord Buddha. In this present time, Maharajji's
devotees have begun to serve in a new era when the
human race has empowered itself with so much
technology to help in transforming the experience of
human life into a truly sublime experience for the
people of the future. The human race is filling planet
Earth and indeed beginning to venture out toward the
planets of our solar system and eventually to the stars.
This explosion of technology is also an aspect of the
inspiration of Maharajji.

Maharajji is a new role model, a new archetype for humanity. Everything about Maharajji is a Lila of Love. To do murder in Maharajji's name is unthinkable. Even the causing of strife in Maharajji's name is unthinkable. Maharajji stands for renunciation. Maharajji epitomizes non-attachment and selfless service to others. Maharajji epitomizes the Love of God, the Love of all that is, all that was, and all that ever will be.

"Maharajji was very much in motion. Before the ashrams were built He traveled very much. And when He stayed in houses, He would frequently change the room in which He resided. And even when He stayed in the same room, He would often change His position where He stayed (and slept) in the room."[65] said Gurudat Sharma.

Maharajji seems to have roamed all over India, particularly north central India. Yet there are stories of Maharajji being in the state of Bihar in eastern India, in south India, in Mumbai on the west coast of India, and others. There is also a story where some devotees of Maharajji flew Him to England for a very short time.

Because Maharajji is like an iceberg, where only 10% of the iceberg is seen, while 90% remains hidden beneath the water, we can never know every amazing story of the deeds of Maharajji. Each story is an indication of what Maharajji did and actually continues to do.

राम राम राम राम राम राम राम राम राम राम राम राम

The Beautiful World

We humans were given (from within) this information technology to see everything that exists in our world. Finally, after many millennia of human existence, there is now a way to begin to understand everything that is going on with the earth. We can understand that there is everything from complete horror to utterly sublime goodness all in this same package. Maharajji is an inspiration to special people to help in this ongoing effort.

The empires of the future will rise and fall. Big things and little things will happen. But to work on yourself is why you are here. Your Jivatma is the core of your work. No one on the outer can fully tell you what your work is. Only you know this. There are literally billions of life stories in the world now. They are only stories. What "we" are doing is amazing. What you are doing is amazing. The work you are doing on yourself can take many paths. We all share many things in common. Devotees of Maharajji are guided to the best path for them whether they ask for it or not. Magic happens whenever "who you think you are" gets out of the way.

Maharajji shows us the beautiful world in all its forms, a world that fits together exquisitely and all individuals play their roles perfectly. Maharajji shows us that there is so much beyond the mundane to be appreciated. Maharajji gives us what we need to take us to the next step. Maharajji is our father and He cares for us with the utmost love. Maharajji plays with us when we are alone and when we are together. Maharajji stretches us to our limits over and over again, and He makes us grow in ways we'd have thought impossible. Maharajji has gotten hold of you, and grace is never withheld.

Mukundaji has written, "...how very gradually and how very confidently Babaji attracted me towards himself. How much he must have labored specially to bring myself to him I being completely devoid of any devotion to God and I who was having such a difficult time and destiny. And, I was actually a complete worldly person full of all kinds of sins and bad actions. Now it was almost like planting, casting seed in a barren land and then to water it and then to nurture it so that it could bring blossoms and some fruit could come out of it. And, whatever went on in the heart of this activity was really a kind of a Lila or a play in which you try to attract a little boy, a boy who is obstinate, you try to entice him by giving him something or the other. But, I had no idea at all at that time nor any kind of wisdom or knowledge that how I, such a foolish person, was receiving the unconditional love and grace and very unique one of such a great and manifested self of the God himself.

"Actually my arrogance was so strong and pride was so strong that it had completely covered all my intelligence, all my discernment, ability to discriminate with things and actually in his own [quote or bhagvad][66] people will be talking about these confusing Lilas or delusive Lilas which could throw anybody off on account of very intellectual and arrogant attitude of those people and there would be constant doubts and constant twisted logic that were offered in order to explain them and actually these doubts and these kinds of twisted logics also used to shake us in our own personal trust upon him. I and my wife will be discussing these Lilas of Babaji which used to be quite confusing to us and we used to battle and really work at it trying to discover the mystery behind these Lilas and the result was very simple that our minds would get more enwrapped into these strange Lilas and the personality of Maharaji and we would never be able to understand what really was the truth behind it. And as a result, we would become more restless. And in this way, we would reach at the apex of this complete inaction not knowing which way to turn and neither we will we be able to throw him out of our lives nor we will be able to embrace him completely."[67]

राम राम राम राम राम राम राम राम राम राम राम राम

Mukundaji describes his first meeting with Maharajji, "Because there was a lot of crowd around his house so out of curiosity I also went in. And there I saw that, on a small tucket, there was a middle-aged, a little heavy-set kind of a person with a little bit sadhu-like dress on him and he was sitting there. Actually, what it was that there was a little lifted up *dhoti*, the undergarment, lower garment, and there was a plaid, an ordinary plaid black and white kind of a blanket. There was a stubble of a beard, his head was a little bald, and he looked like a lost person or a mad person or crazy person kind of person and he was surrounded by the devotees. When I asked who he was, I came to know that he was Baba Neem Karoli. This was a very strange name, but I also saluted him. I sat there for some time and during this whole meeting he was speaking in small small sentences and very mildly and very softly and he was sort of smiling. I was looking at his face and I found it very pleasing to my heart then I got up and left the place. And that very year, our Lord, Shri Baba Neem Karoli Maharaj actually went and gave his darshan to my future wife as I came to know later on. But, this was something that occurred in our life and it just remained there. There was nothing really important about it."[68]

In 1990, Daniel G told me the story of how he first met Maharajji. He said that he was one of many European kids who went to the Himalayas to "challenge God" to provide for them, by going barefoot and carrying almost no possessions. He said that he was walking alone on a mountain trail when he saw a group of people wearing white clothes coming on the same road in the distance. He didn't want to meet them so he left the trail and went up the hill for quite a ways to hide behind a big rock. He was peeking at them as the group was passing well below him. Suddenly the group stopped and one young man from the group climbed halfway up to his position and called for him to come down. Daniel told them he would not come down and to go away and leave him alone. The young man went back to the group. Then he climbed up even closer to Daniel and told Daniel to come down, that Maharajji wanted to see him. Then Daniel came down and accompanied Maharajji's group to Kainchi Ashram. At the ashram, he was given food and then was taken to a house in Bhowali where he was told to stay. He said it was a big house but he only took a small corner of one room to make a sleeping area. Over the next few days, Maharajji sent many young Westerners to stay in that house, until it was full. Daniel had challenged God and God found him. To this day Maharajji still takes care of Daniel, even in America.

I have talked to a number of devotees about the first time they met Maharajji and the last time they were with Maharajji. Just a few examples. Saraswati described how she went to see Maharajji for the last time in His office[69] in Kainchi. After pranaming to Him as He sat on the tucket, she said that when she came up a huge wave of love swept over her. Shivaya Baba told me that the last time he was with Maharajji, He spun around and kicked Shivaya in the middle of his chest pushing him back against the door. Shivaya felt nothing but a profound blast of Love flowing from Maharajji to him. I asked this of Bhagavan Das and after a moments reflection he fell to the ground before me and looked at me in a way I'd never seen before. His face was filled with love and awe and reverence. After some time he said, "That's what it was like."

राम राम राम राम राम राम राम राम राम राम राम राम

The Gods Are Deaf

I heard that Mataji told someone to yell at Hanumanji in the temple if they believed that Hanumanji was not hearing them. This is to get His attention. Hinduism can indeed sometimes be a very loud practice. It has often been said, "The Gods are deaf." So many loud bells and gongs are employed during Hindu pujas. Saraswati, who was with Maharajji in India in the 70s, many years later, said that sometimes she gets very angry with Maharajji and goes into the temple room and fights with Maharajji when she feels He is not taking care of her.

You may be a devotee of Maharajji, but if you think of Maharajji as your Guru, then you have every right to demand that He take care of you, that He provide for you, that He help you. This means that you must sometimes take action. In fact, Maharajji sometimes forces, pushes you, goads you into action, or even reaction. Maharajji doesn't want you to be a "bump on a log." You may have to "flip out" sometimes.

You can throw a fit with Maharajji. You can refuse to eat if He doesn't listen to you. You can "nuke your puja table," so to speak. You can really flip out. You can do whatever your own unique relationship with Maharajji has developed for you to communicate with Maharajji. You can starve yourself refusing to take food. You can "go into your cave" (as men tend to do more than women) until Maharajji brings you out again. You can become so angry that your head spins around with smoke coming out of your ears (as I have seen women do). I feel that such action is a bhakti sort of thing, though perhaps not in any traditional way. You can increase your austerities and intensify your kirtan and puja practice.

Radha Rani from Taos one day got so angry with Maharajji that she removed all the Maharajji photos from our house. She felt that Maharajji would not hear her and was not taking care of us. She was letting Him know it. I was out in the yard using a big weedeater. After some time, I took a moment to rest to get out of the hot sun and drink some water. As I passed by our Honda Element, I noticed that the small window behind the driver's seat was smashed out. It was the window of the car that had a photo-sticker of Maharajji on it. I was shocked that Maharajji had "helped" her by removing the last remaining photo. Sure, it was only a synchronicity. I'd clearly caused that. Yet it was not me. A series of events lined up for a long time to cause that. That event took all the steam out of Radha Rani's anger. Maharajji had revealed Himself. After 2-3 days many photos of Maharajji were back in place throughout our house..., and the window in the car was replaced along with a new photo sticker of Maharajji.

Bhagavan Das narrated the following story in his book, "A man came to see Maharajji because he had only one rupee. The man said, 'Maharajji, this one-note rupee is all I have - I need more.' 'Give me your rupee,' said Maharajji. He took the man's rupee and put it in the fire of his cooking stove. 'What are you doing? That's all that I had!' screamed the man. Maharajji took a pair of tongs, and I watched him pull numerous one-hundred-note rupees out of the fire and give them to the man."[70]

राम राम राम राम राम राम राम राम राम राम राम राम

Maharajji wants you to be happy within. Even in the midst of defeat, Maharajji wants you to be happy – happy at your deepest level - within your Jivatma. I have literally demanded that Maharajji prove to me that He has not abandoned me, so I have "thrown a fit" in some way that indeed brings a result.

This is not about faith. In a way, this is about loss of faith. When you are feeling or thinking that Maharajji has gone away and that you are no longer within His Lila of Love, this is time to demand of Maharajji that he respond to you and to "prove" to you that He is there and to make His grace, His Lila real to you again. People say they do not ask things of Maharajji, but I demand this of Maharajji and He never has let me down. He is God and God loves me.

As I've previously written, I demand that He makes His Lila so clear to me that even a dummy like me can totally understand that He is with me and that He will not forsake me. I demand "signs" and synchronicities, and Lilas. For many years, He has never failed to do this. I am not saying that Maharajji is going to let a child like you and me control Him. He is like the master child psychologist, and we are babies. What more can you be with your all knowing bodiless Guru?

This can mean literally anything and everything that you can do to get Him to hear you. This does not mean that you ask all the other people to help you or solve your problem or prove something to you or do what you want. You must focus on Maharajji exclusively. It is all about Maharajji and you (whomever you really are).

I don't feel that you can demand that Maharajji give you riches and jewelry and even power, because I have never demanded these things of Maharajji. But probably you can ask for those things with satisfactory results. Those things are the same as anything else. If that is what you are to have, then surely Maharajji will open the door for these to flow to you. Indeed, there are many of Maharajji's satsang who live very well.

राम राम राम राम राम राम राम राम राम राम राम राम

In 1996, in Vrindavan, over a stay of several months, it became my habit for several weeks to walk from Maharajji's ashram to the Yamuna River. Dressed in a *lungi* (cloth wrapped around waist), a *kurta* blouse, and sandals, and sometimes smoking charas, I was completely transported out of current time as I traversed the medieval setting. On the second day, I noticed a sadhu carrying a bamboo stick that was perhaps 18 inches long. What a great stick! I deeply desired one of those sticks for myself. On the third day, I reached a particular turning point near the river where I would go to the place I sat in meditation on the riverbank for an hour or more each day. Today there was something different. There in the center of the path was an exact version of the stick I had desired the previous day. I was shocked and looked in every direction in the very rural area by the river. No people were to be seen anywhere. Maharajji had fulfilled my desire and had delivered my stick. I was deeply touched by this little tiny thing that seemed so big to me. After Maharajji gave me the stick, I felt like I was transported from present time, beyond medieval time, and back to the time of Lord Krishna thousand of years ago. I carried the stick for the remainder of the months in Vrindavan and brought it to Taos.

Writing in "I and My Father are One," author Rabboo Joshi describes the following: "Physics dreams of Grand Unification which will explain the formation of the universe to perfection. This is yet to be realized. But such master has a key to your unification with him. He has granted this to you by inserting a chip without your knowing it, merely by a glance, a touch or embrace. In other words, you are bugged for life. He keeps tabs on you throughout your life and helps you achieve your material and spiritual yearnings. Although he can grant you the boons without any karma on your part but he wishes you to work out your karma yourself. Karma has bondage too. All your past lives you have been accumulating karmic bondage, but when you meet your master, in this very life you will be freed of your cumulated bondage of karmas."[71]

When the bible talks about "He that openeth and no man shutteth and He who shutteth and no man openeth"[72], I think of Maharajji. Maharajji is there to open the doors that appear shut to you to increase your positive good in this life. He is there to shut the doors that should be shut to keep you from the detrimental forces of the physical plane and to use His "evil destroying" powers to protect you.[73] So, knock yourself out with your relationship with Maharajji. But remember your laser-like focus on Him is the key. It's all play in the Lila of Maharajji, so "play with it." You are Maharajji's "kid." You're allowed to play with your Father.

राम राम राम राम राम राम राम राम राम राम राम राम

Playing with Time

There are many anomalies surrounding Maharajji, not the least of which is the question of time. Timing is Everything. Synchronicity is a big element of the Lila of Maharajji. Devotees of Maharajji often share these stories with each other. These often reveal how Maharajji uses timing. For example, when two of His devotees meet in such a way that what they both intended to do changes. These meetings can be when people will be at a particular spot within little tiny time windows of 1 or 2 minutes, and sometimes just 1-2 seconds. Often Maharajji will make you late or cause you to be ahead of schedule. There are many stories of this in the daily lives of His devotees. These stories will rarely be written in books about Maharajji's Lilas because He had touched them each in their own very personal way.

Being on time is so strange. I've grown to rely on Maharajji to handle the time. I have a way different sense of how to deal with it than I did when I was younger. There are so many stories of Maharajji's perfect timing. I'm always trying to hear Maharajji about timing – like when I should make a shift, when is the best time to call? I am looking to get the "hit." Because of this, when I've done this correctly, I call someone and they say, "Wow. You called at the perfect time." Then there are the times when I've tried dozens of calls to a person over several days with no answer.

This I attribute to Maharajji, as well – "Oh, Maharajji doesn't want me to talk to that person." Then some time later, I realize that it was good that I didn't plug in with that person for one reason or another.

The timing of Maharajji is mentioned in stories of Maharajji's Lilas. The man who wanted to leave the ashram to bring his fruit to market, only to be delayed by Maharajji, later discovers that if he had taken the fruit to market he would have lost money, but because Maharajji delayed him, he was able to make a profit at a different market. The couple who were to take the train, but Maharajji delayed them, causing them to miss it, later discover that there was a train crash with many people killed in the particular train carriage where they would have ridden.

When they were bringing Maharajji to the train, for example, He made them rush so much and then they would arrive with a long time to wait at the station. Sometimes, Maharajji would suddenly take the rickshaws, on which they rode, off on some side street to give darshan to a man in his home. When the devotees said they would miss the train, Maharajji told them the train would be delayed. Of, course, the train was delayed, and of course, Maharajji's party reached the train station at the perfect time. Maharajji, also, seemed to be able to stand on the platform at the exact spot where the door to His compartment would line up.

राम राम राम राम राम राम राम राम राम राम राम राम

Those Who See that Maharajji Creates the Circumstances Are Graced.

In January 2001, I had been staying in Vrindavan for some weeks and traveling daily to Maharajji's birthplace, Akbarpur, bringing along the pandit for the ceremonies and an 18 year old woman from Taos named Parvati (Jillian). I had been shooting the function for a video that was later posted online. We were the only Westerners there among about fifty thousand Indians yet we felt profound bliss amidst the throng. The following week, Parvati needed to go to Delhi but was unfamiliar with that city, so I brought her there to make some arrangements for traveling back to America some weeks later.

Parvati had been in India for many months. As a reminder that the West even existed, I took her to the Western style restaurant named Nirula's that was on the outer circle of Connaught Place near the Palace Heights hotel, a place once used extensively by Maharajji's satsang. After we had finished and were walking down the stairs of the restaurant, I got an overpowering urge to go walking before getting back in the car. We headed toward the inner circle and I went off, a little to the side, to tell my driver, Rup Singh, that we were going to walk, while Parvati went ahead.

As I was catching up with Parvati, I noticed her ahead in the crowd hopping up and down with joy. As I caught up with her, I saw my very dear friend Krishna (Connie) sitting there paying her fee for an auto rickshaw. She said that she had been at Maharajji's ashram in South India and had just then arrived from the train station. She said that she had taken her bags to Palace Heights and had returned for only 1-2 minutes to pay the auto rickshaw driver.

I asked, "Are you going to the *Maha Kumbh Mela*?" She said, "Oh, I don't know. I was thinking about it, but it is not clear." I said, "Well, we are going back to Vrindavan in two days, then driving to Allahabad to attend. You must come with us." Parvati and I went to Krishna's room at the hotel and spent some quality time with her until evening talking and hanging out.

The next day we did errands in Delhi and the following day we all drove to Vrindavan where we spent one night, then drove to Gurudat Sharma's house in Kanpur where we spent the night. The following morning we drove in my car to Allahabad accompanied by Gurudatji and his wife also named Krishna.

We arrived at *Lal Makan* (red house) the house Maharajji built on Church Lane where Dada and Didi resided for so many years. Several young women from Taos were there at the house preparing to go to

Maharajji's camp at the Kumbh Mela. We spent several wonderful days there before I had to go back to Vrindavan with my car.

Everything changed when we met Krishna on the sidewalk in Delhi. It was much easier for all of us when we were together and Krishna's knowledge of India and her help in making arrangements turned out to be a total boon from Maharajji. All three of us to this day fondly remember this special time because of Maharajji's impeccable timing in New Delhi.

Many devotees talk about the timing and synchronicity in these sorts of rather simple circumstances. It is fun having some chai and listening to Maharajji's devotees speak about impossible meetings, with perfect timing.

राम राम राम राम राम राम राम राम राम राम राम राम

"Often one goes for one thing and finds another," as expressed by Maharajji can be a navigational device in guiding devotees on the path of life. It opens you to the broader picture of your own actions. This means something as simple as, you went to town to the food market, a rather mundane thing, and because you were in town you just happen to run into someone who gives you a job that sustains you through the next two years. It also means that in every action you become aware that there are often other aspects besides the item you initially focused on. Going to Maharajji's ashram to specifically "see" Him, and then finding that so many beloved friends have also come to see Maharajji. Going for one thing and finding many beneficial others. Thank you, Maharajji.

राम राम राम राम राम राम राम राम राम राम राम राम

Maharajji Chooses His Devotees

Maharajji was walking with some devotees in Vrindavan when they passed men leading a herd of goats. One of the men was smoking a chillum (hashish and tobacco blend smoked in a cone shaped clay pipe). Maharajji stopped the man and said, "Who are you?" The man replied, "Who are you?" Maharajji repeated, "Who are you?" to which the man again replied, "Who are You?" Maharajji said, "I am a sweeper" (a low caste) (Maharajji was actually a Brahman). The man said, "I am a goat herder" (a higher caste than sweeper). Maharajji asked the man for a puff on the man's chillum. As the man held out the chillum, Maharajji hit the man on his forehead with His palm. Then He took the man into a nearby ashram and had him bathed and dressed in holy attire. The man was then given initiation and taken to an ashram in the mountains.

Some years ago in Vrindavan, I was told this story about Colonel McKenna. The colonel did not like sadhus or any sort of Babas. Maharajji went into his house when the colonel was not at home and went to his bedroom and sat on the colonel's bed. The Indian servants could not prevent Him from doing so. When Colonel McKenna returned home, the servants told him that Maharajji was there. The colonel was very angry and rushed to his bedroom to abuse Maharajji. Maharajji simply looked at the colonel and must have beamed him with so much love that the colonel changed immediately into a devotee. The colonel stopped his bad attitude toward sadhus and later was promoted to General McKenna.

An old story, recounted in "Barefoot in the Heart," illustrates Maharajji's ever-so-subtle approach. "My father had a Muslim colleague who constantly made fun of him because my father was so enthralled by Baba-ji. He used to say, "I cannot believe that you are taken in by these frauds. This is all mumbo jumbo anyway and I am surprised that someone as intelligent and scientific as you is taken in by these people!" My father used to tell him that since he was not asking him to believe, he should leave him alone. One day, Baba-ji was in town and this colleague said to my father that he wanted to tag along and meet the person who could make a fool of someone so intelligent as my father. They went to meet Baba-ji. As soon as they entered the room, Baba-ji looked at this gentleman and said "You forgot to wear your tabeez today. You should never do that again." (A tabeez is a small [...] locket that is worn around the neck by Hindus and Muslims alike). The man put his hand on his chest and turned pale. He turned to my father and told him that when he was a small child, once he was critically ill. A Muslim priest had given him this tabeez and told him never to take it off because it would protect him. This was the first time that he had forgotten to wear it – He had left it in the bathroom that morning and forgot to wear it after his shower. He became a devotee from that day."[74]

Maharajji will do whatever it takes to pull His devotees to him. I recently heard this story in New Delhi. Kabir was living in Almora many kilometers past Kainchi high in the foothills of the Himalayas. He was hanging out with the sadhus and chillum babas and He didn't like Maharajji. He referred to Maharajji as a "roadside baba" who was nothing but a fake. One day Kabir was bitten by a cobra and was in a life threatening condition. He was brought to Kainchi to Maharajji. Kabir was healed and he never left Maharajji. Till this day Kabir is one of Maharajji's most beloved and influential devotees. Because of Kabir's excellent grasp of Hindi, he often acted as Maharajji's translator to the English speaking kids who came to Maharajji.

"I first met Maharajji in Bhowali many years ago. Maharajji frequently visited a certain Ma's home there. I told her that I had heard about him but had never met him, and I asked her to tell me the next time he came. After a week or so Maharajji came at night. In the morning a message came for me and I went at once. I found him lying on a cot. He looked at me, then closed his eyes for a moment. He knew at once who I was, who I had been before, and what I was going to do in this world. In a few seconds, he said, 'I am very pleased to see you,' which he repeated many times. Maharajji had walked from Nainital to Bhowali during the night. He said, 'You have brought me here! I shall see you again in Haldwani.' Then Maharajji boarded a bus for Almora. (In those days he travelled mostly by bus, not by car.) People warned me not to take him seriously: 'Neem Karoli is a big liar. He very seldom tells the truth. You can't depend on him.' In any case, I went to Haldwani. After a few days someone came to my room and told me that Maharajji had come to Haldwani and gave me his address. I saw him then and have been with him ever since."[75]

राम राम राम राम राम राम राम राम राम राम राम राम

Kabir Das brought the cassette recordings of Maharajji to me to convert them to digital. One day I was working on this project in my studio and a couple young devotees of Maharajji named Shem and Ariana came in. Ariana went over to a shop across the way and Shem took a seat and hung out waiting for her. I said, "Would you like to hear Maharajji speaking?" He said, "Sure." He put on the headphones and listened for a while with an amazed look on his face. We were talking when Ariana came in. I handed her the headphones saying, "Here, listen to this." After listening for a minute or two she asked, "Who is this?" I said, "Maharajji." She then listened deeply and intently for quite a while. When she took off the headphones, she had the look of a person who was completely blown away by the experience. She said, "This is so strange. Two days ago I took the photos of Maharajji off my puja table because I was thinking 'how can Maharajji be my Guru if I have never heard His voice?'" She was almost in a state of shock. I was blown away. When I told Kabir Das about this later, he was also blown away.

राम राम राम राम राम राम राम राम राम राम राम राम

Often there can be a multiplication of signals from Maharajji. Sometimes you can go weeks without any "signs" from Maharajji. At those times you might begin to be concerned about this. Perhaps Maharajji has abandoned you. Then suddenly many synchronistic events, multiple items at once, come apparently out of nowhere within 1-2 days to give you all sorts of indications that Maharajji has not forsaken you at all.

राम राम राम राम राम राम राम राम राम राम राम राम

A Western woman named Uma who served on the Board of Maharajji's Taos Ashram is married to Vish who was with Maharajji in India in the '70s. Uma is a devotee of Maharajji and served Maharajji in so many wonderful ways for many years, although her Guru was not Maharajji. More than 20 years after her days in university, her old roommate, came to stay with her for some days. When her roommate arrived, the roommate saw one of the many photos of Maharajji in her home and said, "Why do you have photos of my Guru in your house?" Uma was amazed that Neem Karoli Baba was her roommate's Guru. The roommate said, "He has always been my Guru. I had a photo of Maharajji in the dormitory room we shared." Uma had never noticed it, although it seems Maharajji was noticing her.

राम राम राम राम राम राम राम राम राम राम राम राम

When you're omnipotent you don't mind being anonymous. Maharajji doesn't care if He is revealed to you or not revealed to you. A lot of Maharajji's workings in your life may not be recognizable except in hindsight. You may have realized that there was an unseen force affecting your life for a long time. Perhaps at the time you thought of this force as an anonymous guardian angel. The Guru always has your best interests at heart. If and when the Guru allows you to know who is the One affecting your life, it is a wonderful thing.

People that can relate to Maharajji have often experienced many lives within this lifetime. Timothy Leary said, "We die so hard each time." How many devotees of Maharajji have had lives they were leading and through circumstances the life just died so that they could not live that same life any longer? Maybe your career as a rock star dried up and you could no longer live as a rock star, but were forced to work as a mechanic for Yellow Cab. Or you lived a life as a mother but your child or children sadly died, and you didn't want more children, so you could no longer live the life of a mother. Suppose you were an excellent athlete and were injured in some way that you could no longer live the life of an athlete. There are thousands of examples of this losing your life and even your whole center of gravity. Yet there is life beyond that life. I have met many devotees of Maharajji who have experienced this. Maharajji has been their lifeline to the next life in many cases.

When you have Maharajji you can no longer ever lose you way, because even in the most dire circumstances, Maharajji stays with you and will remain your center of gravity as long as you are in your body..., and beyond.

I was once at a Ram Dass retreat at Lama. I was complaining to Victoria that Ram Dass had not talked to me or acknowledged me and that I had no individual time with him. A few minutes later we were all standing in a very large circle holding hands. Someone was doing some sort of guided meditation and then there was a prayer. Someone entered the circle a little late and took my right hand. When I opened my eyes five minutes later, I caught Victoria's eyes across from me. She flicked her eyes to my right and I looked and there was Ram Dass holding my hand. After the circle, Ram Dass and I talked for a bit. I totally forgot my unhappiness. Maharajji satisfied my complaint within minutes, and I was happy.

राम राम राम राम राम राम राम राम राम राम राम राम

The problem with writing about Maharajji's effect in our lives is that so much of it is utterly subtle.

राम राम राम राम राम राम राम राम राम राम राम राम

Practice

Maharajji isn't necessarily about puja or aarti. Aarti was done TO Maharajji. Gurudatji told me the following Lila story.

Maharajji and Gurudat Sharma were in Bareilly and they were staying at the ashram there. A group of local Mas[76] was in the habit of doing aarti to Maharajji at the ashram each day. But today Maharajji was not at the ashram. He was with Gurudat a couple of kilometers away sitting by the side of the road.

After a while, the Mas heard about Baba-ji's location and came and wanted to do aarti to Baba-ji right there by the side of the road. He would not allow this and sent them away again and again. Maharajji said it wasn't right that they would be doing aarti is this fashion right there on the road. Still they came back again..., and again. Gurudat told Maharajji that he didn't think that these Mas were going to go away until they had done aarti to Him, as was their practice.

Maharajji relented and the Mas were very happy. They had no matches to light the *buti*[77] for the aarti lamp. They asked Gurudat, who replied that he did not smoke, so he had no matches. What could be done? Finally Maharajji took the buti in His hand, held His hand high in the air and in thirty second or so the buti was aflame. Thus these Mas were able to do aarti to Maharajji.[78]

राम राम राम राम राम राम राम राम राम राम राम राम

Maharajji did, however, encourage very many devotees to practice singing the Hindu bhajans. Practice is done twice daily in all of Maharajji's temples. Practice is done in the homes of Maharajji's satsang. This practice varies somewhat in the homes but practice is very similar in all of Maharajji's temples. There are more than 30 practices pieces that are sung in Maharajji's temples.[79]

राम राम राम राम राम राम राम राम राम राम राम राम

Kirtan

Maharajji's satsang isn't like an organized institution such as Iskcon, for example. There is no hierarchal structure. There are no courses of study. Everything is based on tradition established around Maharajji for many years and sustained in Maharajji's ashrams and temples in India and America, as well as the families in individual homes. Maharajji's satsang is actually a dharma in this sense. Practice involves aarti, kirtan, performance of various pujas, as well as daily seva duties.

The traditions of Maharajji's ashrams in India are mainstream Indian along the lines established by Maharajji. Bhoskar, manager at Maharajji's Vrindavan Ashram, one day told me that Maharajji said, "You pray daily," and that the same tradition is upheld in the proper fashion in all Maharajji's ashrams.

The practices of America's Taos Hanuman Temple at Neem Karoli Baba Ashram are a reflection of the established practices done by Maharajji's temples in India.

In particular, twice daily aarti consists of Jaya Jagadish Hare[80], Hanuman Chalisa[81], Hanuman Ashtoka[82], Vinaya Chalisa[83], Guru Stotra[84], Jaya Gurudev, and Sri Ram Jai Ram. On Sundays, 11 Hanuman Chalisas are sung in praise of Hanumanji. On Tuesday evenings, kirtan is sung consisting of "Sri Ram, Jai Ram," "Sita Ram," and "Hare Krishna Hare Rama." These are according to the tradition of the satsang from the very beginning. Other kirtan singing to God occasionally consists of *bhajans* (Hindu devotional song) to Lord Shivaya, Lord Krishna, Lord Vishnu, and sometimes specific others.

In the *Kali Yuga*[85], kirtan (singing the Holy Names of Gods) is the preferred practice among Maharajji devotees. The Western devotees believe in singing "Hanuman Chalisa" for every reason.

राम राम राम राम राम राम राम राम राम राम राम राम

Maharajji said, "Constant repetition of God's name, even without feelings of devotion, in anger or lethargy, brings out his grace. Once this is realized, there is no room for any misgivings."

राम राम राम राम राम राम राम राम राम राम राम राम

The following is an excerpt from "Pilgrim of the Heart" audio series by beloved kirtan walla, Krishna Das: "The words of these chants are called the divine names and they come from a place that's deeper than our hearts and our thoughts, deeper than the mind. And so as we sing them they turn us towards ourselves, into ourselves. They bring us in, and as we offer ourselves into the experience, the experience changes us. These chants have no meaning other than the experience that we have by doing them. They come from the Hindu tradition, but it's not about being a Hindu, or believing anything in advance. It's just about doing it, and experiencing. Nothing to join, you just sit down and sing.

"Satsang is where people gather together to remember, to turn within and find their own inner path to the One. When we gather together to sing like this we are helping each other find our own paths. We all must travel this path by ourselves because each of us is our own path. All these paths wander on in their own way, but in truth we are all traveling together and until the last of us arrives we will all keep traveling. So let's sing!"[86]

राम राम राम राम राम राम राम राम राम राम राम राम

Jai Uttal, the master musician of kirtan said this: "Kirtan is the calling, the crying, the reaching across infinite space — digging into the heart's deepest well to touch and be touched by the Divine Presence. Kirtan is singing over and over the many names of God and the Goddess, the multi-colored rainbow manifestations of the One. It is said that there is no difference between the name and that which is being named, and as the words roll off our lips in song, the Infinite is invoked, invited, made manifest in our hearts. Kirtan is part of an ancient form of Yoga known as Bhakti, or the Yoga of Devotion. But in Bhakti we redefine 'devotion', we expand the meaning to include every shade of color in the palette of human emotion, turned towards God through song, dance, and worship. These chants have been sung for millennium by sages, sinners, devotees, and the great primordial yogi alchemists of old. And, as we sing, we touch the spirits of the millions of people across the centuries who have sung the same songs and cried the same tears. As we sing, we immerse ourselves in an endless river of prayer that has been flowing since the birth of the first human beings, longing to know their creator."[87]

Maharajji's temples in India have a much larger aarti program and all Maharajji's Indian ashrams have temples for each of multiple deities. In Vrindavan and Kainchi Ashrams, Kirtan Wallahs sing "Hare Krishna

Hare Rama" throughout every day beginning at morning aarti and ending at evening aarti.

राम राम राम राम राम राम राम राम राम राम राम राम

Hanuman Chalisa

When Westerners set out to learn the Hanuman Chalisa so that they can sing it by heart, I have suggested to many that it is a process of "nonlinear learning," unlike learning a song with English words. The process usually takes a long while, sometimes through years of repetition both alone and in groups. I've always been amazed how quickly some of the young devotees have learned excellent versions of Hanuman Chalisa. Through the timeline of the song, there will be little verses or phrases that will "stick" so that when you are singing with the group, you realize that you are indeed remembering it.

Phrases like Verse 37: "*Jai, jai, Jai Hanuman gosahi, kripa karahu avai sada bavai*" ("Victory, victory, victory to Lord Hanuman!, Be merciful even as is the Divine Master"), or Verse 17: "*Tumharo mantra Vibheeshana maanaa, Lankeshvara bhaye saba jaga jaanaa*" ("Vibhishana heeded your counsel, and became Lord of Lanka, as all the world knows") or Verse 22: "*Saba sukha lahai tumhaaree sharanaa, Tuma rakshaka kaahu ko daranaa*" ("Taking refuge in you one finds all delight, those you protect know no fear") may be remembered before other parts. The repetition of the piece is the key. After singing Hanuman Chalisa 108 times you will know (remember) several bits of it. After 1008 times you may remember it all. Imagine after you have sung it 10008 times surely you will be remembering it all by heart in every cell of your body.

Westerners often think that the Hanuman Chalisa is a "prayer," but it is not. Hanuman Chalisa is an "invocation." The Chalisa is sung to call Hanuman to become more present in His murti body with your song of loving praise and the offerings of food you have placed before Him. How wonderful that He will come to you. Hanuman quite naturally reads the minds (the unspoken prayers) of all the devotees present. The same can be said about the Vinaya Chalisa and the other practice pieces.

राम राम राम राम राम राम राम राम राम राम राम राम

Maharajji said, "Saints did Jap (japa) and Sadhana for 10,000 years…, only then they could succeed in Jap, Meditation and Yoga. But people want to be expert within 5-7 months only." This can be applied to your learning of the Hanuman Chalisa as well as other practices. Correct repetition over a long period of time is the key.

One other aspect of this practice bears noting. The devotees are singing the Hanuman Chalisa to please Hanuman and to please Maharajji. By extension the choirmaster (i.e., director) is Hanuman or Maharajji. It is not up to the singers to judge whether their singing is "good." Just let the Gods control you. There are millions of Hanuman Chalisas sung daily throughout the world. Just open your heart and sing and all will be okay. And do not be shy or timid or hold back. You Gods want to hear you.

राम राम राम राम राम राम राम राम राम राम राम राम

Vinaya Chalisa

The Vinaya Chalisa (forty verses in praise of Neem Karoli Baba) is now sung by all devotees of Maharajji's satsang twice a day at aarti. This was not always so. When the man[88] who wrote the Vinaya Chalisa had the darshan of Maharajji for the first time he was so moved that he went home and wrote the verses. When he later brought it to Maharajji, Maharajji refuted it, said it was garbage, tore it up, and threw it on the floor. The devotees naturally gathered the pieces when Maharajji wasn't looking, taped them together and copied it, and some time after Maharajji left His body, distributed it to devotees. Now the Vinaya Chalisa is sung everywhere. Maharajji is such a rascal.

राम राम राम राम राम राम राम राम राम राम राम राम

Puja

Hindu Puja is like dialing an 800 number to God. You have to do it right. That's why Maharajji gave the Westerners in Taos a Hanuman to serve and worship because our beloved Monkey doesn't demand absolute perfection. Hanumanji is a bit more forgiving and minor mistakes receive a loving smile for us all. Yet if you do not do the pujas correctly, you have less chance of getting the direct connection. This is why *Brahmins* are so very fastidious in their application of Hindu practice. When you do it correctly, you have a very direct connection to the God because the *pukka*[89] quality and purity of your practice did not place any hurdles or blockades in your path. Brahmin *pandit*s and pujaris are taught for many years and study on their own for many years, too. Theirs is a life of deep devotion to the performance of pujas and the singing of bhajans, for the benefit of all.

Virtually every devotee in Maharajji's satsang that I ever met has a puja table in his or her home. These pujas are generally focused on Maharajji, Mataji, Hanuman, as well as any number of *shaligrams*, *yantras*, and various images of Hindu deities based on the lineage and inclination of the devotee. Because of Maharajji's appeal to Jews and Christians and Buddhists and Sikhs, it is not uncommon to find a menorah, or image of Christ or Buddha, or Sikh Guru. Some of these home puja tables are huge, even taking up as much as a whole room. In India, there is a puja set up in every home, store and office, and in fact all new houses in India are designed with a temple room.

However, Maharajji didn't insist you do puja, and in fact might thwart your participation in puja ceremonies. It is all His play. Gurudat Sharma told me that he very much wanted to conduct a puja and *yugna* on a certain Hindu holy day. He pestered Maharajji to let him lead the puja. Maharajji relented and told Gurudat he had permission to do this. The puja was begun with Gurudat leading. After 15-20 minutes, Maharajji called Gurudat to come sit with Him on the side and that is where he stayed for the remainder of the puja. Perhaps Maharajji wanted to break Gurudat's attachment to performance of such pujas, although Gurudat surely participated in a great number of pujas thereafter.

राम राम राम राम राम राम राम राम राम राम राम राम

Remembering Maharajji

I've tried to remember Maharajji every minute. This is, quite naturally, impossible. Yet it is possible to bring your attention to Maharajji during the course of your day. Pausing to thank Maharajji, or to ask for direction or ask what to do or even just to repeat Maharajji's mantra "Ram Ram Ram Ram" over and over. This is very helpful. It is very helpful in remembering that Maharajji is there with you. By extension, Maharajji encouraged us to ask Ram. No matter what is happening, you can pause and take a breath, repeat Ram Rams and remember Maharajji..., and feel His love.

राम राम राम राम राम राम राम राम राम राम राम राम

Maharajji said, "By taking the name of Ram, everything is accomplished."

राम राम राम राम राम राम राम राम राम राम राम राम

Maharajji isn't about meditation. In fact, when devotees tried to mediate around Maharajji, He sometimes did things to interrupt, annoy and interfere with them. There is a story in one of the books where Maharajji told a group of young Westerners to meditate, then He began telling jokes and making everyone laugh. Yet Ram Dass seems to have had a very high meditation in the presence of Maharajji.

Maharajji said, "See all women as mothers, serve them as your mother. When you see the entire world as the mother, the ego falls away."

When a young Western devotee living in the ashram began taking care of a cat giving it food and letting it stay in the room, Maharajji said, "Here I am telling you to give up attachment, and now you have become attached to a cat."

Most of the Westerners were with Maharajji for very little time overall. Some devotees, who were effected for their whole lives by Maharajji, were only physically with Maharajji for 15 minutes ever. Some were able to be with Maharajji for months. The Westerner kids who were with Maharajji were quite young - most were in their early 20s. Look at their faces in the photos. Maharajji touched each one so deeply. Most, if not all, had amazing lives. It appears that it only takes a nanosecond of Maharajji's darshan presence for you to be graced.

राम राम राम राम राम राम राम राम राम राम राम राम

Guru - Guruism - Guruist

Hinduism is very complex. In fact, Hinduism is as complex as the whole of existence. This is quite natural considering the reported 3.3 Million Hindu Gods (some claim 33 million). Neem Karoli Baba existed in a Hindu world and Maharajji's family are Brahmins, but He did not teach Hinduism, at least not to the young Westerners who came to Him. He is God manifest in form. He is the Supreme Being. Maharajji is not necessarily a "Hindu Guru." Maharajji as "the Guru of Gurus" is the "Global Guru" or "Universal Guru."

I consider myself to be a "Guruist" in that my principal devotion and worship is to my Guru, Maharajji Neem Karoli Baba. Many of Maharajji's Western satsang are actually Guruists. They love and serve Maharajji as their Guru. They are cared for and guided by their Guru. This form of Guruism is not something that Hindus or anyone else much talks about in the Hindu world.

However, there are Gurus in many lineages of Hinduism. Many are among the greatest people to walk the earth.

It is very easy in this extremely complex world of Hinduism to lose sight of Maharajji because He is so very subtle, yet it has been said that every lineage of

Hinduism bows to and touches the feet of Maharajji as a manifestation of Bhagwan.

Guruism is very simple. All the complexities of Hinduism are summed up in one phrase used often by Maharajji, "Sub Ek," or "All One" in English. All *Deva* and *Devi*, all lineages, all practice, all forms, all doctrines, indeed all people are all one thing. To accept a fully realized being is to accept that He is that one thing. Maharajji was a Guru who appeared in form. Now, Maharajji is a Guru who does not necessarily have the form we saw him in for many years. According to Maharajji, He was going to be in a new body and that we would not recognize until He was ready to show Himself again.

Maharajji goes beyond the person we call Neem Karoli Baba.

राम राम राम राम राम राम राम राम राम राम राम राम

Maharajji said, "Whatever may be Guru - he may be a lunatic or a common person. Once you have accepted him, he is the lord of lords."

राम राम राम राम राम राम राम राम राम राम राम राम

Guru of Gurus

Maharajji has plucked so many out of mundane existence and shown them a wonderful perspective on life as well as provided a path of wonderment, miracles and Lila's upon which to traverse this lifetime.

A number of years ago a wise man in India told me that as "The Guru of Gurus," Maharajji's job is not to make *chelas* (spiritual students). Maharajji's job is to make Gurus. I have contemplated this for years and have observed that to be true.

While the word is being used to describe a non-spiritual pursuit, for example "economic guru," "entertainment guru," or even something like "plumbing guru," the Gurus that Maharajji makes are indeed spiritual. As Maharajji guides His devotees along the spiritual path, these devotees in turn help guide "newer" devotees on the path to Maharajji, perhaps in effect allowing Maharajji to be a guide for the other through their own open heart. These people act in varying ways as exemplars with their *Yanni* yoga, Bhakti yoga, open hearts and lack of ego, and help to remove the darkness of ignorance from others.

Guru seems to be one of the most abused words now. It is used everywhere for such mundane things. Yet, it is only natural that this should happen. Earlier the word Guru was certainly known by only a few in the West, but it basically began to proliferate worldwide when Ram Dass began to speak, in ever widening circles, of Maharajji as a Guru. It seems that the word is charged with so much energy that it has caught on in unexpected ways. Guru is a God word. Almost all other uses of the word are but watered down worldly versions of what the word actually means.

Several of the Westerners who were with Maharajji have been Gurus to me in some manner through the course of many years. They have profoundly and permanently affected my outlook on life and helped me remain focused on the path. In the "big picture" there is no specific lineage in Maharajji's satsang, no office holder in the supreme sense that has been appointed to the "position."

Many devotees who were with Maharajji in body have wonderful things to impart about the wonders of Maharajji, in their own ways, to help enlighten and inform those who will follow. And this indeed goes on because Maharajji was actually working more on the inner than on the outer. It is Maharajji's grace that He is using a new way in the world - from heart to heart - spreading the knowledge, the truth, and the Love.

राम राम राम राम राम राम राम राम राम राम राम राम

Maharajji Bhaktis

Perhaps you might simply call us "Maharajji Bhaktis" because we are love-intoxicated devotees. Maharajji is our personal *Ista Devata* (*Ishta Devata*)[90]. In bhakti, faults are not seen by God.

Regarding Bhakti: In Valmiki's Ramayana, Ram describes the path as ninefold (*nava-vidha bhakti*):

"Such pure devotion is expressed in nine ways. First is satsang or association with love-intoxicated devotees. The second is to develop a taste for hearing my nectar-like stories. The third is service to the Guru (...) Fourth is to sing my kirtan (communal chorus) (...) Japa or repetition of my Holy name and chanting my bhajans are the fifth expression (...) To follow scriptural injunctions always, to practice control of the senses, nobility of character and selfless service, these are expressions of the sixth mode of bhakti. Seeing me manifested everywhere in this world and worshipping my saints more than myself is the seventh mode of bhakti. To find no fault with anyone and to be contented with one's lot is the eighth mode of bhakti. Unreserved surrender with total faith in my strength is the ninth and highest stage. Shabari, anyone who practices one of these nine modes of my bhakti pleases me most and reaches me without fail.[91]

Hanuman Das told me that in the 1990s he met an old Baba in Chitrakut who said that in 1929 he went to a sadhu's cave in a mountain valley named Kainchi[92] in the remote foothills of the Himalayas where some nine hundred sadhus had gathered to take the darshan of and to receive the blessing of a fully realized being. That being was Baba Nib Karori, known later in the

West as Neem Karoli Baba. This happened at the site where Maharajji later got the Kainchi Ashram built. This event is surely not the only time a gathering such as this happened around Maharajji.

राम राम राम राम राम राम राम राम राम राम राम राम

Who can imagine what Maharajji's satsang will be like in 100 years? Only Maharajji knows. Maharajji has pulled so many people to Him since He left His Neem Karoli Baba body. His Lila has continued. It is sheer grace when those who have entered into His Lila can identify who is causing this Lila.

Maharajji sent many devotees to other Gurus and teachers. Maharajji wasn't throwing them out. He was just directing them to the one who had the most to teach them. I heard of one case where Maharajji told one Western devotee that Ram Dass was his Guru.

राम राम राम राम राम राम राम राम राम राम राम राम

Maharajji said, "We meet only those people with whom our meeting is predestined. Duration of association with each person is also preordained. One should not grieve if one is separated or if the association does not last long."

राम राम राम राम राम राम राम राम राम राम राम राम

See God in Everything

Maharajji said to simply "See God in Everything." If you really see God in everything then perhaps you will understand that your life is most likely predetermined, and remaining with it long enough, you will know this predetermination of your life as a certainty. Why would it matter one way or the other? It doesn't. Your life is passing with every revolution of the planet, with every trip around the sun. Your life begins and your life ends. Then another life begins and that life ends. Your Jivatma knows all these other lives. When you get closer to your Jivatma, you get closer to the beautiful truth of this three-dimensional physical plane of existence.

Rajida writes, "God exists in all aspects of nature, his creation. He is everywhere so is never out of our sight. The fault is ours if we are not able to see him or do not earnestly try to see him. We must not limit our vision. The narrow tendencies of the mind keep us so entangled in mundane activities that we are not aware of him. Our impure thoughts prevent us from achieving peace of mind and divine love."[93]

Maharajji's India

If you become enthralled with Maharajji, it is a good idea to go to India to visit His ashrams and temples. This will help you put Maharajji into a cultural, historical, vibrational as well as spiritual context. That sounds simple but it isn't. However, travel to India has been an important part of the growth of most of the Western devotees who have come after Maharajji's time. India is a land of saints and sages. There is much that will deeply touch you spiritually in India. It is good to stay as close to Maharajji as possible in India.

Alan Watts[94] said, "Jesus Christ knew he was God. So wake up and find out eventually who you really are. In our culture, of course, they'll say you're crazy and you're blasphemous, and they'll either put you in jail or in a nut house (which is pretty much the same thing). However if you wake up in India and tell your friends and relations, 'My goodness, I've just discovered that I'm God,' they'll laugh and say, 'Oh, congratulations, at last you found out.'"

राम राम राम राम राम राम राम राम राम राम राम राम

India Yatra

Traveling to India on a budget is not something to be taken lightly, but it is very possible. India is absolutely filled with people. Adequate cultural and spiritual study and mental preparation must be undertaken before traveling to India but it will certainly be worthwhile if you do. For those who make a pilgrimage to the places of Maharajji, and immerse themselves in the study of Maharajji's Lilas, and the practices inherent in the Maharajji "scene" in India, nothing can ever be quite the same for them again. This is not to be taken as some sightseeing trip, or photo op, or buying spree, or vacation. Sure, those things can happen. No problem. But for the pilgrim immersed in Maharajji, a new world emerges.

Just so you know, Indians speak English a bit differently than Americans. For your first India *yatra*[95], you will find that many Indians speak English. However, English in India often uses different English words and phrases than you might be used to. There are so many variations that a whole book could be written on the topic. As an example, the word "mental" when spoken by Americans, connotes functions of thinking and such things as perhaps mental telepathy. To the Indians, the word mental means more of an insanity, like in mental institution, or in thinking too much to the extent that the person has out-of-control thoughts. Another example is Indians refer to "marriage" and do not seem to know the word "wedding." So, please keep your eyes open and your ears open, too. And remember that you cannot expect Indians to understand many of the Westerners slang words and colloquial phrasing that are common. The best thing is to try to use English as it was taught in school.

If you are fortunate to be allowed to stay in one of Maharajji's ashrams, the best idea is to adhere strictly to the ashram routine. This means you would get up at sunrise, bathe, take chai, attend morning aarti, hang out, study holy books, meditate, or do seva, take lunch at the prescribed time, take rest in the afternoon, take chai at 4:00 pm, attend evening aarti, take food at the evening dinner hour, retire to your room, sleep. Then next morning begin to spend the day in the same way. This is the basic schedule of the daily routine of all of Maharajji's ashrams. In fact, this is the basic schedule of most of the ashrams in India. Spending some time as an ashram inmate is a good way to calm and center and recharge your batteries.

राम राम राम राम राम राम राम राम राम राम राम राम

Why Was Maharajji in India?

You might wonder why Maharajji was in India rather than in the West during the Lila of Neem Karoli Baba. Maharajji said, "India is a land of Saints and Sages." It is that simple. For one thing, India has always cherished and encouraged the natural healers, the great spiritual teacher seers, and of course the Gurus. On the other hand, in The West, if you showed the slightest inclination toward independently having the power of healing, or talked with spirits, or if you did divination, or deviated from the Catholic church, or anything out of the ordinary in some positive way, you were killed – hung, burned, chopped – by the church itself. There is ample evidence of this.[96]

I feel that the West is just too dangerous a place for saints and sages. The West is a very "worldly" place. Modern Western culture constantly spins out an endless stream of things to take you off any sort of real spiritual practice. And in this case, I mean the spiritual path of awakening to your true nature. Almost every single thing on television, for example, is about a "happening" that is not happening to you. It is a world of spin and the distraction of often useless talk and meaningless actions, and often downright fabricated lies.

Of course Maharajji was in India, because at the very least India has the DNA of the beings with higher powers that the Western churches were wiping out in Europe. Maharajji said not to teach by differences, but if you look deeply, you will see that there are apparently vast cultural differences. This is not to say that India is better than the West (Europe, America, Australia), nor is the West better than India. Americans are fundamentally really good people. They were the first on Earth to live in a country where the masses were given freedom to wander around anywhere, do any sort of work that they were capable of doing, discuss and criticize the government and indeed actively participate in government. But the world changed tremendously in the two hundred fifty years since the American experiment began. The world is in apparent chaos everywhere, yet it is controlled chaos. Maharajji let us find Him in a magical environment far from the pressures of life in the West. Maharajji is everywhere. But He gave His grace to India, and He let His Lila play out in this way for us.

राम राम राम राम राम राम राम राम राम राम राम राम

Ashoka the Great

The greatest ruler ever in the world is probably the Emperor Ashoka of India. He was the first and only ruler to establish a totally nonviolent state some 350 years before the time of Christ and about 150 years since the time of Buddha. Ashoka was a warrior king who ordered the killing of many, during his wars of conquest toward building an Indian Empire. One day Ashoka went to a battlefield shortly after a battle. He was aghast at the horrible aftermath – the blood, the gore, the death of so many innocent people.

He was so thoroughly disgusted that he became a Buddhist. It was Emperor Ashoka who sent out thousands of Buddhist monks into the world with instructions to preach the gospel of nonviolent Buddhism to everyone. The Emperor's conversion to Buddhism changed him from "Ashoka the Fierce" to "Ashoka the Great." Ashoka governed by issuing many decrees. The most important were carved on stone columns erected in many areas of the countryside. In the state established by the Emperor Ashoka, things changed. For example, the emperor forbad most of the killing of animals for food, and the quantity of animals killed dropped to below 10% of its former level.

Ashoka established *Ahimsa*, which means "to not injure" in Sanskrit, and was first described in *Rig Veda* (around 1700 BCE) in the phrase, "do not harm anything."[97]. On the current flag of the nation of India, Ashoka's *Chakra*, a wheel with 24 spokes is displayed. "Chakra is a Sanskrit word which also means 'cycle' or 'self-repeating process.' The process it signifies is the cycle of time - as in how the world changes with time."[98] Of course, the peaceful empire established by this ruler who became enlightened lasted only some 30-40 years, but it did provide a sort of prototype for a peacefully governed nation and national philosophy of peace. Maharajji said, "India is a Land of Saints and Sages."

राम राम राम राम राम राम राम राम राम राम राम राम

"I Build Beautiful Temples"

Maharajji said, "I build beautiful temples so that people will be attracted to them and eventually fall in love with the God that resides within."

Temple or *mandir* is the dwelling place of God. It is a quiet place used primarily for meditation, prayer, worship and the utmost care is needed to maintain its sanctity.

In the delightful book "Prem Avatar," Mukundaji writes about Maharajji's ashrams. "Maharajji's devotees who deserved His Grace have been innumerable, extending from Kashmir to Kanyakumari, from Punjab to Assam and even in foreign countries, even though He had not founded any institution with the purpose of organized satsang by His name. Wandering sadhu, today here, and tomorrow somewhere else. He was never attached to any temple or ashram. A few years before leaving His body, He got management of the temples and ashrams systematized with the purpose - (1) that after He had left His body, the devotees who entirely depended on Him should have something to lean on and (2) to fulfill His wish that in the thick of *Kaliyug*, the spiritual feelings be awakened in each and everyone through these temples/ashrams.

"He never permitted His name to be associated anywhere with them, but having founded them once, He got the Hanuman Trust formed and handed them over to it. It is only after His *Mahaprayan* (final journey) that His devotees added His name to the temples/ashrams.

"He had one principle, one laudable attribute and purpose - the welfare of each and everyone. Therefore, all people - high or low caste Hindus, Muslims, Christians, Sikhs, Jains and even foreigners were recipient of His grace."[99]

When people think of "us," they are usually thinking of an organization that is an institution. "We did it." Like that. This can signify a national, local, corporate, or even tribal identity. The "us" can also refer to a temporary team. With Maharajji's satsang, there is no institution that governs the satsang, no institution that passes new rules. There are individual ashrams and temples dedicated to Maharajji that are organized as institutions only out of necessity.

Maharajji Had Many Rules

Ushaji told me one day, "Maharajji had many rules and He enforced them strictly." It is those rules of Maharajji's that are upheld as traditions. The traditional practices are the general rules. She said that Maharajji controlled every aspect of the ashrams, even the tiniest aspects. For one thing, He knew everything. He knew about all the supplies of food, milk, water, blankets, ghee and He could manifest needed items in some miraculous way as needed.

An example of this is told in the story of His Lila with the leaf plates that no one had thought to obtain for the big bhandara. At the end of the day, everyone was sitting around Maharajji thinking that everything was 100% prepared for the huge bhandara the following day. Maharajji asked how they planned to serve this massive amount of food to the people. Only then was it discovered that leaf plates had been forgotten. There at the temple, late at night, with no hope of obtaining leaf plates to serve, Maharajji caused them to appear out of the darkness when a caravan was seen in the distance. The owners were carrying their loads to the market on the backs of donkeys. The donkeys were loaded with leaf plates.[100]

Ushaji went on to tell that after Maharajji left His body, no one knew how to operate Kainchi Ashram on a daily basis. A group of six senior devotees travelled to several of India's most respected ashrams and interviewed the managers about their methods of ashram management. Then they selected the best, most fitting, of these methods to operate Kainchi and other Maharajji ashrams. This is, of course, also the Lila of Maharajji, because He controls everything even till this day. Maharajji caused the devotees to manage the ashram using studied, logical, and tested approaches. The management Lila's of Maharajji did not end, but there was now a baseline for daily operation.

राम राम राम राम राम राम राम राम राम राम राम राम

Sacrosanct Tradition

Tradition is an absolute must in Maharajji's ashrams and temples. New ideas are not needed. Yes, there are situations that appear to require minor adjustments, but really these are just all under the umbrella of what Maharajji demonstrated to us all. The organization IS Maharajji, our unseen, always felt, always-in-control Guru. As in the temples within the ashrams, the practice, the songs sung and chants done and aarti performed are of a certain type to ensure the vibration of the ashram is as Maharajji demanded. So too the operation of the daily life of the ashram is covered by the very simple traditions established by Maharajji. This was demonstrated over the course of many years as to the means of feeding large groups, as well as handling, identifying, and jaoing antisocial elements who might pollute the atmosphere and intention of the ashram.

Maharajji has created all this for us and it is sacrosanct. It therefore behooves a person who is new to the ashram to study and observe the operation of the ashram and to fit in with the traditions of the ashram. As Baba Sharma, manager of Maharajji's Delhi Ashram, said, "Observe the seva that others around you are doing and then join in this seva in the same way they are doing it." There is no other MahaGuru necessary within the ashrams of Maharajji. As was indicated previously, Maharajji is the Guru of Gurus, and in many ways the inmates and visitors are a form of lesser or greater Guru, but none supersede Maharajji in even the smallest way.

The leader of satsang is only Maharajji. He does this through His Lilas and through inner communication with each individual devotee. This certainly does not mean that when it comes to His ashrams and temples, what Maharajji tells you is "how it is." This could be a position on some issue that Maharajji wants you to take in the moment. Maharajji may have internally instructed another devotee to take an opposing position on the same issue. He will play it out as He wills, so you will not become attached. Serve Maharajji without attachment.

When visiting any ashram you should leave your thinking just outside the ashram gate. Let Maharajji do all the thinking and just open your heart to Maharajji, to the other devotees, and to the practice. An important purpose of the ashram is to calm your thinking. Let it happen and fill your mind with Maharajji and Maharajji's love.

There is no organization beyond each individual ashram, except for Maharajji. One must trust the decentralized nature of the world that is revolving around Maharajji. It is not necessary for you to attend the ashrams or temples of Maharajji. If He calls you then you must come. If He does not, then that affects nothing.

Temples Are for Everyone

Maharajji was here to help the downtrodden. "Once Babaji went to Hanuman temple, Lucknow by Kehar Singh's car. Umadatta Shukla also was with them. Babaji went into the temple and facing Hanumanji sat by the fence on the road-side. The driver also desired to have Hanumanji's darshan. Therefore, he locked the car and went into the temple by the bridge at the side of the road. When Shuklaji saw him he came running and met him half-way on the bridge and jostled him out. The Supreme Being' Babaji, though He had His back towards them saw all this. He came running and set the driver free with such force that Umadatta could not bear the push and fell on one side. Admonishing Shuklaji He asked, 'Who are you to stop him? Do you think I have built this temple for you? It has been built for them (low castes, poor, miserable and afflicted).' Saying so He took that *Koiri* (a low caste), holding him by the hand, to Hanumanji and bending His head made him to pranaam Hanumanji. Kehar Singhji was an eye-witness to this incident."[101]

EVERYONE gets jaoed (sent away) at some point. And that's okay. Gurudatji told how "Maharajji jaoed many people. VIPs would come and get their ladhus (a sweet) and they would want to remain with Maharajji. But Maharajji would snap His fingers and point for them to go. If they hesitated for even one second, He repeated the command in a stronger way. This happened even with VVVVIPs. Maharajji didn't care if you were rich or famous."

राम राम राम राम राम राम राम राम राम राम राम राम

At these ashrams the topic is Maharajji. Devotees often forget this and begin to think it is about them and their own topics. Yet Maharajji uses so many subtle methods to always guide these devotees on their own special spiritual path. Devotees may not fully understand that they will not get lost. This is because of His love for them. In time, they all come to realize that Maharajji has profoundly affected their lives.

Usha Bahadur narrated the following story about Maharajji's policy about *bakar bat* (useless talk) at His ashrams. "Some young people were at Kainchi Ashram[102] fooling around and talking loudly about their own things and interests, their own business. Maharajji stormed out of His room yelling at them and chased them right out of the ashram. They ran out of the ashram and Maharajji ran right after them yelling all the while. Even right across the bridge, He chased them. Maharajji said the ashram is not a place for the worldly thoughts and that the ashram was a place where your heart and your thoughts were able to become one. That to go and stay at an ashram for a year was a way to 'recharge your batteries' and that after that you could go back into the world and do your work again, in the right way. This is why Maharajji had many rules and enforced these rules very strongly."[103]

Ashrams are places of quiet, contemplation, introspection, inner practice, theological study, and meditation. Public ashrams most always have public temples. Temples are places of occasional large crowds at festivals and many Hindu holy days when crowds gather for pujas and yugnas. There is often much noise and commotion and activity at these times, which are the opposite of the purpose of the ashram. This is a dynamic that mirrors the nature of the world.

Maharajji's pandit, Gurudatji, spoke to me of the organization of Maharajji's ashrams saying, "Integration - cooperation in all things is good. Disintegration - with no cooperation, things fall apart. Without integration, you don't deserve the Guru's grace."

Feed Everyone

During video shooting we were doing at my home in Taos, Ram Dass, Balaram Das, Krishna Das, and Sita Sharan were discussing Maharajji's feeding of devotees at the ashram. Ram Dass said, "I've wondered why He fed us so much." Sita suggested, "I think He did it to put us to sleep because all the subtle work was done while we were sleeping," and added, tongue in cheek,

"The drugs were in the food." All laughed and agreed, although there were no actual drugs.

Prasad is something that has been blessed by a saint. Anything that Maharajji has blessed and given to you is prasad. Everything from Maharajji's hand is prasad. You take Hanuman prasad at the Hanuman temple, Shiva prasad at the Shiva temple or sadhu's *dhuni*, for example. Prasad means "a gracious gift." Grace is in the prasad. All the way past the molecular to the nano particle level, prasad is good for you. Prasad is never refused. If you do not wish to partake of the prasad, you must receive the prasad and then pass it on in some way. Anything properly prepared and offered thing that comes to you in Maharajji's name can be prasad.

राम राम राम राम राम राम राम राम राम राम राम राम

Usha Bahadur told me that Maharajji said, "It is entirely against the tradition of the ashram that someone should get away without being given food."

राम राम राम राम राम राम राम राम राम राम राम राम

Bhandara

Bhandara means to literally open the storeroom and eat everything there, but of course a lot more than just one storeroom's worth of food was served. Maharajji said that God comes to starving people in the form of food. The blessed food that Maharajji serves is filled with a tremendous vibration of love and well being.

It has been said that the bhandara for the *pranapratishta* (inauguration) of the Paniki Hanuman murti and the temple in Kanpur UP India[104], Maharajji fed the entire city of Kanpur. This is a bit of a stretch, but clearly there must have been a huge multitude that Maharajji caused to be fed that day.

It may be closer to reality when it was said that at the bhandara for the opening of Maharajji's Vrindavan Ashram on *Parikrama Marg* that Maharajji fed every schoolchild in Vrindavan.

Even till the present time, Maharajji's Kainchi Ashram feeds from 100,000 to 125,000 during the Pandra June Bhandara (June 15th), which celebrates the anniversary of its opening.

It was said 50,000 people were fed on one day in January 2001 at the bhandara for the pranapratishta (inauguration) of the temple at the site of Maharajji's birth in the tiny agricultural village of Akbarpur UP. I was in attendance that day and can attest to the tremendous number of people who were fed throughout the all-day bhandara.

It seems that if you want to make Maharajji happy with you, you feed others whenever possible. This can be as simple as serving chai to everyone who visits your home or as large as having your own bhandaras in your home to serve "offered food" for many guests. The key is that all food served in Maharajji's name is offered to Maharajji first for His blessing and then the food is distributed to everyone, as prasad. This offering can be overt and rather elaborate, or the offering can be covertly subtle, such as remembering Maharajji in your mind and silently repeating Rams.

In the ashrams, simple food is served daily. Meals consist of *subji* (some boiled vegetable with some boiled potato), *dal* (a form of lentil soup), *roti* (flatbread, also called chapati), and *chawal* (rice). Sometimes *khir* (sweet rice pudding) is served. And a real treat is *mirch* (hot pepper) or *acchar* pickle.

At bhandaras a wider variety of food is served. There can be 3-4 vegetable dishes, *puri* in place of the *roti*, *laddhus* might be given as the sweet Prasad, and in the case of very large bhandara, *malpuas*.

Chai is served constantly in India. Chai is made from ground tea, water, milk, sugar, ginger, and cardamom. In India, the Western satsang mostly drinks "Special Chai," which is made with only milk, no water, for obvious reasons. Ginger has heating properties. Cardamom has cooling properties. During cold time, the quantity of ginger would be larger and the quantity of cardamom would be less. During hot time, larger amount of cardamom (a full pinch, perhaps) and a rather smaller quantity of ginger would be used (perhaps only 20-30% of the winter dose). The perfect chai is more than a beverage. It seems to be medicinal, and indeed a boost to some spiritual practice. Venode Joshi told me that Maharajji never took sugar in his chai.

This is a glimpse of the tradition of food service at Maharajji's ashrams and temples.

राम राम राम राम राम राम राम राम राम राम राम राम

Vrindavan Ashram

When I arrived at Maharajji's Vrindavan Ashram many years ago, Kabir Das was living there with Kamala. On my first day there, Kabir said, "You are in your father's house, act as you would in your father's house." This was one of the deepest and most memorable things I ever heard regarding Maharajji and His ashrams.

Some areas such as Vrindavan have experienced tremendous growth since the time that Maharajji established His ashram there in a very peaceful rural area on *Parikrama Marg*[105]. On certain days, particularly Holi, the Parikrama, which is a road that is used by pilgrims for circumambulation of the holy city of

Vrindavan, more than a million people will pass the front of Maharajji's ashram. Yet it is in Vrindavan where one can feel an irresistible presence of Maharajji. Maharajji chose Vrindavan as the place where He left His last known body and this ashram is the place of His *mahasamadhi* temple. Vrindavan is arguably the holy city of Hinduism and the center of the Bhakti Movement of God intoxication. Vrindavan is located beside the holy Yamuna River and has some 5,000 public temples that are among the holiest in India, a country filled with holy temples. I was told that there are an estimated 50,000+ private temples in Vrindavan, as well. Thus, circumambulation of some 55,000+ public and private temples in Vrindavan is a very auspicious thing. Devotees staying at Maharajji's ashram often begin and end their parikrama outside the gate of the ashram.

Usha Bahadur narrated to me that, on one *Vasant Panchmi* (celebration of the first day of the Indian spring season), Maharajji came to her house in the morning and made telephone calls to various people all over India non-stop all day. She was amazed that she never received any bill for this excessive phone calling. Because of this Lila of Maharajji, some time later, it was Ushaji who, remembering this day, suggested that the pranapratistha (inauguration) of Maharajji's mahasamadhi temple in Vrindavan, in 1981, be performed on the day of Vasant Panchmi.

Maharajji's son, Dharma Narayan, told Radha Rani that Maharajji had given him many instructions about running Maharajji's Vrindavan Ashram. Maharajji told him that Vrindavan did not have the usual ashram rules. He said that at this ashram, inmates would have more freedom. They could go shopping, or not go shopping, do aarti, or not do aarti, eat the ashram food, or not eat the ashram food, visit outside Saints, or not visit outside Saints, etc.. It is up to them.

राम राम राम राम राम राम राम राम राम राम राम राम

Kainchi Ashram

Kainchi, on the other hand, has experienced only a little growth, still retaining the small scale and very shanti qualities that are the reason His ashram was established there. Westerners are often drawn to Kainchi for the small but profoundly deep Durga Festival in the Fall, as well as the huge bhandara on June 15th. From Kainchi it is reasonably easy to access such places as Kakrighat, Jageshwar (where they have been doing Pujas to Lord Shiva several times a day, every day for a thousand years), and Chota Char Dham[106]. On the other side of Kainchi, are temples established by Maharajji at Hanumanghar and Bhumiadar, some 30-38 km distance.

राम राम राम राम राम राम राम राम राम राम राम राम

Bhumiadar Ashram

After Maharajji's first temple at Hanumanghar, near Nani Tal, was built in 1965, Maharajji didn't go there much. Bhumiadar is a very small ashram and Hanuman temple that Maharajji used as His base of operation, so to speak. It is not so far from Naintal and Kainchi Ashram. Maharajji liked to visit the village of Bhumiadar on Gethia-Bhumiadhar road. Maharajji did not have a room there but slept outside anywhere that he wanted. When His devotees discovered that Maharajji was there, they often came to visit Him and held bhandaras and pujas and did aarti to Him. A devotee gave a small piece of land by the roadside and a small *kutir* (hut) was built. Then later a temple was built. It is from this place that Maharajji would go out to the surrounding areas. Bhumiadar Ashram is a delightful place to visit at times, and other times it is not possible to enter. Mataji sometimes stays there and gives Her darshan.

राम राम राम राम राम राम राम राम राम राम राम राम

Akbarpur Janambhumi Temple

Visiting the temple to Maharajji at His birthplace (*janambhumi*) of Akbarpur about 38 km southeast of Agra can be a very deep experience. This tiny agricultural village, surrounded by potato fields, is much the same as such Indian villages have been for hundreds if not thousands of years. Lakshmi Narayan Sharma, who we know as Neem Karoli Baba, has a large family there and was once headman of this village for a time. Maharajji's family has established a school for girls in this village.

राम राम राम राम राम राम राम राम राम राम राम राम

Other Ashrams

There are also Maharajji ashrams in Rishikesh, Shimla, Kanpur, Lucknow, a house in Allahabad on Church Lane, as well a tremendous number of small Hanuman temples established by Maharajji. I was told that Maharajji established over 108 Hanuman temples widely scattered throughout India. Maharajji established Hanuman temples in Nib Karori in UP, Bavania in Gujarat, and Kakrighat on the road between Kainchi and Jageshwar.[107]

Taos - Beautiful People Everywhere

We've noticed over many years in Taos that the longer devotees are with Maharajji, the more beautiful they become. It is very subtle and very wonderful to watch. Maharajji opens the devotees to a different reality and the effect can be seen on their faces as time goes by.

The temple may be the most visited Hanuman mandir in North America. People from all over the world come to Taos for Hanumanji's darshan. And here it is in a very earthy, tiny resort town and artist colony, far from the mainstream.

Taos is the "seat" of Maharajji in America. So many thousands of persons come to Hanumanji and Maharajji to offer prayers, engage in puja such as kirtan and aarti, offer thanks, pray for guidance and deliverance. Everyone who comes to Maharajji in Taos is always given just what they need and when they leave they always take the next step on the perfect path for them. This could be a new job or relationship, or ending a relationship, or a new sense of order in their own lives.

राम राम राम राम राम राम राम राम राम राम राम राम

The Taos Ashram[108] itself is rather more of a "Guruist" establishment dedicated to Maharajji Neem Karoli Baba. The ashram is not necessarily Hindu, although it upholds Maharajji's standard for service and compassion for all. What IS totally Hindu, however, is the Hanuman Temple within this ashram. This temple is home to Sri Taos Hanumanji, a very large approximately 750 Kg (1654 lb.) murti (sculpture) of Lord Hanuman in his *Ramachudamanipradayaka* (Deliverer of Ram's Ring) form. Although Taos Hanuman is depicted as flying, He is not in the *Sagarotharaka* (Leapt Across the Ocean) form because He is holding Ram's ring as He carries it to Sita in Lanka. The murti, which is the embodiment of the Living Hanuman, was sculpted in Jaipur, India and brought to America by Maharajji's devotees.

This Hanuman temple in America was created in Maharajji's name for the worship of Hanuman by Hanuman believers among the Westerner devotees, and by the thousands of Indians in America who make pilgrimages to Taos Hanuman, The Lord, to receive His blessing and His grace whether they are familiar with Maharajji or not. The honor of serving these Hindu Indians has been given to the Western devotees who are inmates or seva volunteers in the service of these visiting Indians in the same way that so many Indians have served the Western devotees in His ashrams in India for so many years.

राम राम राम राम राम राम राम राम राम राम राम राम

Shivaya Baba, Jagdish, and Jai Ram many years ago spent several hours one day listing the 108 unlisted rules of Taos Ashram. These all turned out to be rules with the word "No" in them. They included such things as: no shoes in the temple room, no bare shoulders in temple room, no tasting of food during preparation, no food is eaten unless it is offered to Maharajji first, no eggs or garlic or onions in food[109], no foods other than strictly vegetarian, no wading in the irrigation ditches, no smoking in the central areas, no dogs, no conflicts, no shoes at the *dhuni*[110], and so forth. These rules for the most part reflect the rules of Maharajji's senior temples and ashrams in India.

राम राम राम राम राम राम राम राम राम राम राम राम

K. C. Tewari was quoted as saying, "Maharajji taught that a temple is a place of God, and should be open to every heart. The cleanliness of the murti and the decoration with colorful clothes are essential for maintaining the purity and the sanctity of the temple and attracting worshipers and devotees. If the people whose duty it was to look after these arrangements do not bother about them, the result is that the temples would cease to be places for purification, and people actually came to be repelled by them. Inner purity cannot come in an unclean and hostile environment."[III] Let every member of our community be responsible for his or her presence within the ashram with the fore knowledge that our purpose is to create a place of love, service, devotion, truth and God. Our constant respect for what Maharajji appreciated adds to the quality of service contributed and to attracting more people to God.

Dancing in the Two

Ram Dass described "living in The One and dancing in The Two." This beautiful phrase means the formless and the formed, as well as that which is unfocused or focused on the physical plane. Getting lost in the world of the two cannot happen because we are eternally living in the world of the One. We only receive a limited time to be here as consciousness focused in physical form (The Two) because the human bodies hold together for such a short span of years. Even Devoria Baba, the great saint who principally resided in Vrindavan had only 250 years maximum. This is a natural, on-going cycle. Understanding this is surely very helpful in realizing how you can live your life while you are here, regardless of the apparent circumstances. Dancing is an "experience."

Maharajji always resides in the one and was dancing in the two in the form of Neem Karoli Baba. He is certainly dancing in the two still, even in His Neem Karoli Baba form, as well as other forms.

With Maharajji as our role model, so to speak, it is for us here now to realize the truth of this reality that our essential consciousness, our Jivatma is always in the one but we are dancing, playing, in the two. It's not at all easy but the more we understand this, the more it benefits us.

We came from the One and we will return to the One. It doesn't take the mind to know this. In fact the mind (which is fully based in the two) will do everything it can to convince you this isn't true. However, it is the ultimate truth, the highest truth..., for all of us. The mind lives to give us mental constructs of how it all is, yet the mind is limited to the two. Maharajji said that you need to have "special eyes" to see God (The One).

राम राम राम राम राम राम राम राम राम राम राम राम

So you're a big businessman and make a lot of money. That's great. Remember the times you needed luck to survive or to win? Who do you attribute that luck to? Do you think that the luck was predetermined or just a random act or maybe it was caused by Lady Luck? How many times have you been lucky? Could it be your karma? Or did you do it all with hard work? Do you attribute it to God? Or to the Gods? To your Guru? Very Good.

In the early '90s I was sitting with a man at a satsang gathering. I asked him how he came to know Maharajji. He told a most interesting tale that illustrates yet another way Maharajji gathered a devotee. The man said that, in the '70s, he had been in jail for his third time because of selling small bags of pot. When he was let out of jail, he needed to make some money so he went back to his old business. He obtained some grass from a big dealer and sold some on the street. An undercover cop, across the street, saw the transaction and was coming after him. He walked rapidly up the street and ducked into a busy bookstore. He grabbed a book from a display without looking at it and stood in the checkout line looking as innocent as possible. It didn't fool the cop who arrested him as soon as he walked out the door. They locked him in jail and took everything from him as usual; but they let him keep the book. The book was "Miracle of Love: Stories of Neem Karoli Baba." As he sat in his jail cell reading the stories, he was completely blown away. He had never even imagined that a person like Maharajji existed. He became a devotee, and later made quite a lot of money in the IT field. He had two sons and a good family life. Later he became quite the gentleman farmer. Maharajji found him and took care of him. "Lucky man," as we say in India.

राम राम राम राम राम राम राम राम राम राम राम राम

The Seen and Unseen

The physical plane created by consciousness contains the seen and the unseen – humans can see things within the perceptions allowed by their bodies, yet it has been said that there are also the astral, causal, mental, and etheric fields of vibration.[112] These too are in the physical plane created by Atma consciousness. However, the four latter levels operate at different frequencies and velocities than the physical level so we cannot see them, although many of us can occasionally perceive them. Many great people have worked with these other unseen levels of the physical plane, yet to believe that playing within these levels is the ultimate answer is to remain trapped in the physical world created by consciousness.

We are aware of these levels unconsciously through our Jivatmas and indeed some adepts use them and draw powers from them. This is pointed out so the reader will understand that we are not speaking of a physical plane phenomenon regarding Maharajji. Please don't become attached to this model of the physical plane. Maharajji did not teach this model. Maharajji is beyond all that. Maharajji's consciousness is connected directly to the highest level, the Atma consciousness through all vibrational levels. Our minds cannot know how. Devotion is not a mental exercise, a mental pursuit. Just realize that it is all Samsara. It all abides in Love. Maharajji is the miracle of Love.

राम राम राम राम राम राम राम राम राम राम राम राम

Chakras, *Kundalini*, Meditation, Yoga, Astrology, Precognition, Telepathy, Telekinesis, Psychokinesis, Tarot, I Ching, Ouija, Ziriya, Channeling ----- these are physical plane things that operate within the other unseen vibratory levels. However, there is a component of some wherein the very highest practitioners achieve a direct connection with the divine beyond even the unseen planes created by consciousness. This is well beyond rare, and actually rather impossible. On the physical plane there is much that is created by the will of the mind in both seen and unseen ways within these other levels.

I recently took part in a Ziriya channeling session when the entity coming through the board claimed to be Maharajji. I took this with a grain of salt. However, the session was powerful and rather informative indeed. If Maharajji wants to send you a message via Ziriya, He will surely guide you to a Ziriya session as surely as He will direct a telephone call to you. It's all His Lila. But it is best to understand that you are connected to Him internally. The Guru is not external.

In the case of astrology, the movements of large bodies in space are affecting everyone. There is no question of that. $E=mc^2$ proves it. Energy equals mass times the velocity of the speed of light squared. There is plenty of mass traveling between heavenly bodies at light speed squared, and you are standing on a heavenly body. It is the interpretation (by astrologers) of this phenomenon which is what can be in question. One would have to trust that the affects of astrology would have been observed, studied, and recorded for many millennia to distill the meaning of the movement of the stars and planets. That is another matter.

राम राम राम राम राम राम राम राम राम राम राम राम

As we all know, many things about the physical plane are absolutely amazing. That is, of course, why it was created by consciousness. We go on and on discovering the physical plane. Yes, that is why it was created and why we continue to take many births. But Maharajji was showing us a calmer, more centered reality within our own Jivatmas, the perfect vantage point from which to view the world.

राम राम राम राम राम राम राम राम राम राम राम राम

Maharajji Speaks Internally

Maharajji speaks internally into a place in your thinking that seems to be different from the place of normal thoughts. Maharajji speaks externally through signs and Lilas. One never really knows who or what is communicating. Those of us for whom Maharajji is Guru see everything as some sort of manifestation of Him, so for us Ziriya, I Ching or the like are but manifestations of His play. Boring day or exciting day - either way it is just a manifestation of Maharajji's Lila. Whether sunny day or rainy day, it is the same. More play of Maharajji. My Radha said one day, "I don't believe Maharajji controls the weather." I said, "Really? Well, I do." Listen, it's all just a holographic illusion. Maharajji seems to have pierced that in some way or even many ways.

Here's one example of Maharajji's control of weather. Maharajji's daughter, Girija, tells the story of when she was a small girl she wanted to sleep on the roof. People in India love to sleep on the roof. She asked her mother if she could. Her mother told her to ask Maharajji for permission. Maharajji said she could sleep on the roof, but if it rained she had to come down. It was a perfectly clear night so Girija happily went to the roof with some bedding and settled down. As she lay there she watched a small cloud begin to appear in the distance. The cloud grew and grew all the while coming closer. By the time it was overhead it was quite dark and began to rain and even hail on her. She had to come down.

It is likely that Maharajji finds us when we have become lost. Or maybe we have got to become lost so that we can find Maharajji. If you are a spiritual seeker, you are looking for something. What could that be? Maybe you have just grown very tired of the trap of commercialism, shallowness, and mindless conformity of the worldly pursuits. Maybe you did well in the world for a long time, maybe you never found much of anything you liked at all. Maybe you silently cried in anguish in some internal way and Maharajji came to you. Whatever or however this came to be does not matter. Maharajji is here for you and you are now in service to Maharajji. You can give it all to Maharajji and

He will give it back to you. Thereafter, you are aware that it is all His Prasad.

राम राम राम राम राम राम राम राम राम राम राम राम

Now You Run It for Me

There is a story in India of a king of a large kingdom who lived in a huge palace. His Guru was a sadhu (renunciate) who lived in a little kutir (hut) beside the palace. One day the king went out of the palace to visit his Guru at his kutir. The king presented a document that gave the entire kingdom to his Guru. The Guru accepted the document saying, "Fine. Now you run it for me." This is the way it works. And you don't have to advertise it to everyone.

I've often felt that regardless of his public words, Steve Jobs did this with Apple. He gave it all to Maharajji and Maharajji told him to run it. It has been suggested that Steve Jobs may never have given to charity, but he gave some of the greatest gifts the world has ever known to all the people of Earth. Steve's companies changed everything for all of us. The sum total of the thing within Steve's lifetime is that he created supercomputers and sold them to the masses often in the guise of a cute little box, then beyond the desk, he virtually transformed the music industry, completely upped the anti for the whole communication industry and utterly transformed the production of animation.

For many years, since I first heard about Steve's connection with Maharajji's satsang, I've believed the "magic" behind Steve Jobs and Apple was Maharajji. Just look at how the whole thing evolved. Maharajji took care of Steve.., all the way. Lo and behold, the young hippie drop-out who stayed, for a time, at Maharajji's Kainchi Ashram, as a spiritual seeker, eventually had billions of dollars in play and billions of people were positively affected.

I feel like Maharajji gave Steve the early concept of Apple and gave him the ideas all along the path, then He took it away (but left him with a lot of money) and set him to work in another area of the game and then He brought Steve back to take the really big step of really taking over a true leadership role in the world. It's all sssooo Maharajji. :-)

राम राम राम राम राम राम राम राम राम राम राम राम

Looking for Maharajji

Devotees of Maharajji are completely enthralled by photos of Him.[113] We just can't seem to get enough of them. Devotees collect Maharajji photographs almost like baseball cards when we were kids. These images of Maharajji fill us with love. We know they are watching over us. I am always more comfortable in rooms with Maharajji photos there.

When Maharajji was here among us, devotees never knew where to find Him. They had to hunt for Him and follow leads like detectives. Maharajji was really hard to track down. Is He in Vrindavan, or Kainchi, or Agra, or Allahabad, or Mathura, or a private home? Where is He? Maharajji said that by remembering Him, He would come to you. So, devotees would have magical meetings with him with unlikely synchronicity, unlikely timing. Even if they managed to get to places where Maharajji was certain to be, sometimes Maharajji actually made Himself invisible. Oh My God! If Maharajji couldn't be seen, how could anyone even know that? They could know that because Maharajji had people with Him who later reported that He also made them invisible. And actually beyond being invisible, they also could not be heard, although people who were right there could neither see nor hear them. Imagine being the person with Maharajji when Maharajji did that. Would your mind have any frame of reference to explain this? It must have been much like being on LSD.

Even now we don't know where to find Him, but He is still here somewhere. Maharajji seems likely to have had several bodies in the times when Neem Karoli Baba was very much giving darshan to the satsang. Plus there is the added claim by some of Maharajji's devotees that He is a time traveler.

We were in Vrindavan Ashram in perhaps 2010. Hanuman Das, Lakshmi, Govinda, Garish from Kainchi, and I believe Satrupa was there, too. After dinner, we were all in one of the rooms upstairs in the back taking chai and hanging out talking about Maharajji. It was lovely relaxing satsang time together. Garish said that during the preceding Kainchi bhandara on June 15th, Maharajji came, IN BODY, to their house across the road from Kainchi Ashram and gave darshan to several people. He further said that he personally had been in the room with Maharajji and had received Maharajji's darshan. We were all totally shocked at this report.

राम राम राम राम राम राम राम राम राम राम राम राम

I look for Maharajji everywhere, every day. I know of many devotees who also look for Maharajji constantly, particularly in India, although Maharajji could be spotted anywhere in the world. Of course, it is a subtle looking. It's not like compulsively looking at every face for a glimmer of Maharajji. I see Maharajji in everybody. I'm talking about Maharajji, the time traveler, in His Neem Karoli Baba form. Have devotees been successful in seeing Maharajji? Yes..., but that's private.

Here is an amazing story of Maharajji's Lila told by a woman from Cambodia. She had been living in a house in a village there. A man would come to visit her regularly over some period of time. He was very nice and she liked him a lot. One day the man came to her house and told her to pack up her belongings and leave as soon as possible because her house was going to be bombed from the sky. She believed the man and left the village. It happened! The next day her house was blown to bits by a bomb dropped by an airplane. Only later in India when she saw a photo of Maharajji, did she realize that Maharajji was the same man who had visited her. She told many people at Maharajji's Vrindavan Ashram about this.

So, yet another anomaly arises. Maharajji said that He would leave His old body and get a new body. However, as has been said, He likely had more than one body because He appeared in two or even more places at the same time, unless this could be explained by time traveling.

राम राम राम राम राम राम राम राम राम राम राम राम

Who Makes the Rules?

There are small Lilas around everywhere, all the time. Jai Ram tells a story, "In the mid '90s, many of the devotees at Neem Karoli Baba Ashram in Taos, New Mexico, USA, smoked cigarettes and bidis[114]. There were few outside areas at the ashram where smoking was not allowed. The custom has now been reversed and there are almost no areas where smoking is allowed, and almost none of the satsang smokes cigarettes or bidis anymore. As a step toward that, the ashram's Board of Directors made a new rule that the area just outside what we call 'Maharajji's office,' often referred to as 'Maharajji's porch,' was now a no smoking area. Still, many of the local devotees refused to stop smoking in that vicinity. I adhered to the rule for some time, but after some months, I began to occasionally smoke there myself. One day perhaps two years after the Board's ruling, I was sitting there in the old rocking chair talking with another devotee. We were just outside Maharajji's double door entrance. That porch of Maharajji's is a wonderful place to sit and it is noted for the wonderful sunsets that can be seen across the field. We were facing toward the field. I took out a bidi. As I lit the bidi, I said to the other devotee, 'They made a rule that you cannot smoke here, but no one enforces it, so I just smoke.' We continued our conversation. After maybe a minute, we looked off to the right toward the vegetable garden. I was holding the lit bidi in my left hand perhaps a foot from my face. As we turned, the bidi suddenly jumped from my hand and flew over and landed directly on the tip of my tongue. It gave me a pain that hurt like anything. I mean it really hurt. My eyes became filled with tears and I could barely say a word for a minute. The other devotee was watching some activity in the garden area and I did not let my intense pain show. It was very clear that Maharajji enforced that rule, Himself. This is why I never smoke anywhere near Maharajji's office and porch area."[115] I've come to realize that Maharajji totally controls what happens at His ashrams (and by extension, everything else. Right?) down to the smallest detail. Again, how is that possible? It is well beyond our reasoning, beyond the thinking capability of our minds.

राम राम राम राम राम राम राम राम राम राम राम राम

Maharajji Seen in USA

This is a story that happened in Taos in the late '80s. This is precisely how this was told to me about a year afterwards. Hanuman Das (HD) was then manager of the ashram. He loaned his car to a devotee to run some errands. In town the devotee ran a red light and was stopped by police. The policeman called in on his radio and discovered that HD had forgotten to pay a ticket. So there was a warrant for him. The policeman said he would forget the red light infraction, if the devotee would take him to HD.

So the police arrived at the Hanuman temple. The policeman came to the door of the house and spoke with HD about the old ticket and said that he had to take HD to the station. It was hot summertime and HD was dressed in shorts with no shirt. He asked the policeman if it was okay if he went to his room and put on some more suitable clothes. The policeman said it was no problem.

When HD returned to the kitchen, the policeman was staring at the large photo of Maharajji hanging on the wall. He said to HD, "Who is that?" HD said, "That's Neem Karoli Baba, our Guru. He left His body in 1973." The policeman said, "What do you mean 'left His body?'" 'Left His body' is clearly not a phrase an American policeman can relate to. HD replied, "He died." The policeman said, "No he didn't." HD said, "Yes, he died in 1973." The policeman reiterated, "No He didn't. I see Him walking in town at night. He wears a blanket and has no shoes. When I try to catch up with Him to find out what He's doing, He always steps around a corner and disappears."

Ram Rani told us that a few years later, this same policeman came to her house because of some minor thing her young boys did. While inside the house, the policeman pointed to the photo of Maharajji on the table and said, "I love this guy."

राम राम राम राम राम राम राम राम राम राम राम राम

Maharajji said, "The great sadhus don't have a human body. They are omnipresent. If a saint changes form, he doesn't necessarily have to take on a human body. The soul is the small form and the human body is the huge form."

राम राम राम राम राम राम राम राम राम राम राम राम

Maharajji in Amarkantak

"A few weeks after Maharajji's mahasamadhi, a stranger came to the Hanuman temple in Lucknow. He said that he knew Maharajji and thought that he was a great soul. The pujari realized that the man didn't know about Maharajji's mahasamadhi. He told him that the urn contained ashes from Maharajji's cremation. The man said that this was impossible, since he had just seen Maharajji a few days earlier in Amarkantak. He said that Maharajji had worn only a burlap sack around his waist and no other clothing. Maharajji had told him that he had left his blanket in Kainchi and that from then on he wouldn't wear expensive dhotis. He had said that ashrams were prisons and that they caused attachment to creep into the minds of sadhus, who were supposed to have cleansed the mind of attachment. Maharajji had said that he had run away from the ashrams and that he'd never return. From now on he would live in the jungle and have time to sing and pray without disturbance. The priest was taken aback by the man's revelations. A moment later he turned to question the stranger and he discovered that the man had disappeared."[116]

राम राम राम राम राम राम राम राम राम राम राम राम

At the pranapratishta of the temple in Akbarpur, Baba C. S. Sharma told me that Maharajji has made it very simple for those who want simplicity. Everything to be known is in the titles of the first three books about Maharajji. If you will 'Be Here Now," then you are doing "The Only Dance There Is." If you are doing "The Only Dance There Is," then you are in Maharajji's "Miracle of Love." You need know nothing more to begin the path.

In Vrindavan, Gurudat Sharmaji advised me that when you are doubting Maharajji is a supernatural being, doubting that He is a manifestation of God, it is because Maharajji is always trying to escape. Do not let yourself be fooled by this ploy of Maharajji.

Mukunda wrote, "Whatever took place was due to Babaji's supernatural power. A person who was not particularly inclined towards Babaji, mutely and motionlessly looked at his face and his Lila. The others experienced inexplicable bliss and felt delighted and elated."[117]

राम राम राम राम राम राम राम राम राम राम राम राम

I'd Run Right After Him

During a radio interview with Radha Fournier, Krishna Das the great kirtan singer who has inspired so many and filled so many hearts with Maharajji's love, said the following:

"Because we're physical beings, and because we are identified with our physical bodies, we seem to think that a Guru, a real Guru, is also a physical body. But it's not that way.

"And even though He has left that particular physical body, His presence is stronger than ever. And for me, He is that presence. You know. He's a living presence in my own heart and when I remember myself, I'm remembering Him. When I'm aware..., I'm aware of that presence that He is; that's what He is for me. It's almost as if He is the air. And the space that we live in.

"And He never goes anywhere. We don't look. Whenever we look, He's there. So, even when we're not looking, He's there. But we don't look. So, my whole spiritual practice is to keep aware and to keep seeing Him all the time. You know. As much as I can. And when the heart is charged up and turned on, you know, that's when you're aware of His presence. That's who He is for me now – become the whole universe.

"If I saw him running down the street, I'd run right after him. I'd leave everything. In a split second. Just because we are not seeing the physical body, doesn't mean there isn't one. He's completely in control of our experience and He is running the show completely.

"When you surrender to a real master, it's only by grace that you surrender. It's not an act of your own personal will. Once surrender has happened, then everything in your life becomes your Guru, your Master, your Beloved. There's nowhere you go that He's not there. There is nothing you're thinking that he's not programming (in a way). Just because He doesn't want us to see Him now, that's because that's just what's best for us. Because the real Guru can only do what is best for you. No possibility. But a real master *Satguru* doesn't have any personal desires left. There is no..., they become the universe. What is there for them to want? Or need?

"So, a real master, a *Bodhisattva*, only can do what's in the best interests of everybody. If we're not seeing Him and the physical body now, that means that's what our best interests are now and we have to accept that completely as the way He wants it. 'Cause He could show up right now in this room, and sit on that chair right there. Who's to say He's not there? I just don't see Him.

"For us, our job is to remember that love, to remember who He is, and to live in His presence as much as we can."[118].

राम राम राम राम राम राम राम राम राम राम राम राम

Maharajji's satsang are, I feel, a special breed of people. Maharajji helps everyone always. Maharajji doesn't pick you if you are not ready. If you are not ready, you simply do not become a devotee. How do you get ready? It takes lifetimes. Of course, if you are reading this, you likely know you've had many lifetimes as conscious Jivatma. It's not just a one-shot deal. Maharajji's *sevaks* (selfless servants) have travelled a long way through time over the course of many lives and many bodies with Him. Maharajji is always adding Guru brothers and Guru sisters to our satsang family, to the cast of characters who serve Maharajji in large and small ways. Not everyone has the capacity to fully "get it," but all are growing.

In this new millennium, the understanding of humans will be different than before. It is almost as if a major mutation in human kind has taken place with the huge growth of the world's population from 1.65 billion people in 1900 to 6 billion in 2000. Yet it is now that the change in humans is becoming obvious. People have much more going for them, not the least of which is a new spirituality-based inner knowing. Soon the kids of the "Baby Boom" will have finished their work and will all depart the scene, leaving this planet very different from when they were born.

राम राम राम राम राम राम राम राम राम राम राम राम

Spirituality and belief have changed in the Western cultures of North America and Europe. The grip of Christianity as a belief structure has been broken in much of that area, while the belief in the truth spoken by Jesus remains and is often revered.

Although the churches have much money and power and adherents, studied individuals have realized that there is a different way to look at spirituality. The movement of the new generation is toward the best understanding of what is at the core of the teaching of the great souls who create peace and love in the world.

There will be those who will say that the example of Maharajji is a "ridiculous fantasy", but that would be untrue. It is through the spread of truth, that the real ridiculous fantasies, perpetrated by many religious leaders, to subjugate the masses are being revealed. It is the spread of truth that will bring the people of the earth to a better understanding of where each of us fits in the all that is, all that was, and all that ever will be. It is among the next generations, those who have been removed from the yoke of ignorance, that some truly great spiritual leaders will emerge.

It is very possible for the mind to create ridiculous fantasies about the unseen world of the physical plane and of the greater consciousness of the "I," but there is no creation that will ever be as wonderful and as true as the reality. To get to that reality is the opposite of creation. That's right. The path to the truth is the opposite of a mind creation. There is no system of creation to explain it all. There is no big organization needed to enforce spiritual beliefs. There is only the growth of the understanding that the old models of religion contain so many ridiculous fantasies that the core teaching of the founders have been buried through the ages by so many lesser beings using their minds to obscure the truth of reality and the nature of our souls.

It is the minds of these lesser beings and so-called leaders that have caused so many wars and massacres and famines and suffering throughout the ages through their illogical reasoning and foolish reasons. There is no organization run by the mind that can stop the wrongness.

The way of the future is that the new people of the world begin to understand en masse that the truth is within them, not in the mind, but in the heart of each and every one of the humans. That is to say, within the Jivatma souls of all the people of Earth.

This is what Maharajji brought to us in His appearance as Neem Karoli Baba. The fully realized master, Maharajji, will always be present among us in one body or another to remind us. We are His children and He will never go away. He is the tiniest and most humble among us and He is so much greater than everything ever manifested on the physical plane.

राम राम राम राम राम राम राम राम राम राम राम राम

Maharajji Knows Everything

Ushaji told Radha Rani and me two stories about what Maharajji showed her when they were in Badrinath. She said that she was looking across to a mountain and saw a huge horse walking there. The horse was so huge that its stomach was higher that the tall deodar trees of the jungle. Maharajji told her that was the horse that Lord Shiva rides.

One night she was sitting with Maharajji. Occasionally little glowing white lights emerged from the mountain and flew off into space. At times, the lights came from space and disappeared into the mountain. Maharajji told her that these were the light-bodies of the yogis in the caves as they went out to travel the universe.

Clearly, Maharajji saw through the Maya of illusion and could show others.

राम राम राम राम राम राम राम राम राम राम राम राम

In Divine Reality, Rajida tells this story of Maharajji's mind reading: "Kishan Lal Sah, a teacher from Ramgarh, Nainital often visited Kainchi to have Baba's darshan. His devotion was such that Baba was both his Guru and God. In spite of his deep faith, Kishan Lal was feeling depressed. He was disturbed by the evil seen in the world and by his own lack of spiritual progress. One day he went to Kainchi with the thought of discussing the matter with Baba. When he arrived, Kishan Lal saw Baba sitting on one end of the wooden bridge over the river. He went to him and bowed reverently.

"Before he could ask anything, Baba said, 'You see others trapped by Maya (illusion). Narada and Bharata were entrapped by Maya. These great sages were entrapped by it, so what is there to say about others?' Kishan Lal felt that there was no need to question Baba further.

"On a different occasion Sah went to Baba with innumerable questions on spirituality. He greeted Baba, who was lying in his *kuti* (room), but he could not think of which question to ask first. Baba selected one important question from the unexpressed ones and answered it without being asked. Baba said, 'This temple and whatever is seen by the human eye are illusion. What can you do about it?' This led to other questions and doubts in Kishan Lal's mind. Baba again answered them without being asked. Baba said, 'Delusion makes everything look real.' Kishan Lal thought that there should be a way out. Baba answered, 'Attachment is only dispelled by grace.' How can one obtain grace, came to Sah's mind. Baba said, 'Constant repetition of God's name, even without feelings of devotion, in anger or lethargy, brings out his grace. Once this is realized, there is no room for misgivings.'

"In this way, Baba satisfied the seeker by giving him simple answers to his important, unexpressed questions. As it says in the Ramayana, "Ram, the embodiment of truth, consciousness, and bliss dispels attachment as the sun dissipates darkness."[119]

The story above is not as simple as it appears. It illustrates something very important. Maharajji knows what you are thinking. He knows all of it, including your inner questions as well as the answers.

राम राम राम राम राम राम राम राम राम राम राम राम

Dwarka told me the following story of Maharajji knowing what a devotee is thinking. A young man was in south India in the early '70s . He was told that at any given time, there are 5 fully realized spiritual masters on Earth who are unknown to anyone, and 5 fully realized spiritual masters who are known to everyone. Later he went to the north of India and was sitting hoping to take the darshan of Maharajji. Maharajji was turned away from the young man and not paying any attention to him, so the man began thinking very much about the 5 known and 5 unknown masters. Maharajji turned and looked at the man. Maharajji held up His fingers one by one – 1-2-3-4-5. Then Maharajji closed His hand and extended 1 finger. Maharajji always said, "sub ek." In Hindi this means "all one." As with each of Maharajji's teachings, we can all have a different take on the meaning of this, but my own take was that Maharajji with this action was saying these masters were actually one..., and I feel that the One Master is Maharajji.

राम राम राम राम राम राम राम राम राम राम राम राम

Around Maharajji there is absolutely no privacy. Everything about you is revealed to Him. He loves you anyway. That's the way it is with God. Everything is known.

राम राम राम राम राम राम राम राम राम राम राम राम

There Is No More Randomness

With a Guru like ours, you realize there is no more randomness, no more chance. If you win the lottery, it is a gift from Maharajji. In fact, there is a story that Maharajji told one Indian couple to buy a lottery ticket and they won. Anything and everything that befalls you is attributed to Maharajji.

Gurudatji told me that if you came to Maharajji with an objective, He would not accept you. But if you were innocent and open and loving, He took you right in. Some people came with an objective or an attachment. As the following story told to Radha and me at Kainchi illustrates, with Maharajji your attachment could have unintended results.

"One very rich woman came to Maharajji with a big box of sweets for Maharajji. She wanted to take the sweets for herself and her friends outside. She held out the box to Maharajji so that when he touched it, the sweets would become prasad.

"Maharajji took the box and the woman would not let go. She held on and tried to pull them away from Maharajji. But he pulled them back and then the woman pulled again. This happened again. Back and forth.

"Then Maharajji pulled so hard that He got the box away from the woman. Then Maharajji immediately said, 'You can go now.'

"The woman was so sad. Maharajji started to distribute the sweets, but Usha said, 'Maharajji, You can't do this. This woman will have a heart attack before she leaves and who will pick up her body?' So Maharajji and Usha watched as the woman left the ashram and walked to her car. When she got in the car and had driven away, only then did Maharajji distribute the prasad. They laughed and laughed so much."[120]

राम राम राम राम राम राम राम राम राम राम राम राम

Swami Rama tells us that he was going around Nani Tal with Maharajji one day visiting the homes of

Maharajji's devotees. At every home Maharajji took food that was offered to Him. At the final home when Maharajji was offered food, Swami Rama told Maharajji that He had already eaten 40 meals that day. He said that Maharajji seemed amazed and didn't realize He had done that. Of course Maharajji realized it (He knew everything) but He could not refuse to take food offered with love by His devotees.[121]

Several years ago in Maharajji's ashram in Vrindavan India, I told my mentor Gurudat Sharma that the day before I had finished reading the *Manu Smriti* and was about to begin studying the Vedas. He said, "There is many a man who burns in hell who has read all the Vedas, but no man burns in hell who has studied the stories of Neem Karoli Baba." Well, that was the end of that. I gave the book to Ram Das, a young Westerner from Taos who was staying at the ashram. Quite naturally, I went back to emersion of my studies of Maharajji's Lilas.

राम राम राम राम राम राम राम राम राम राम राम राम

Everything in India is secret, hidden behind the smokescreen of 3.3 million gods. It is said that most Westerners can never really know. Being born a Hindu is the only way.

राम राम राम राम राम राम राम राम राम राम राम राम

Meek Shall Inherit the Earth

There is so much war associated with the religions of the Middle East. There is almost constant conflict. It has been that way since biblical times, so it's all so very serious. Devotees of Maharajji find that everything around Maharajji is very light and loving. War is not an issue. Half the time, people around Maharajji were laughing and crying with tears of joy. The conflicts that arise come from the uncooked seeds within some devotees or the individual karma that had to play out within the satsang environment. These certainly did not amount to anything like war. In the time of Neem Karoli Baba, India was in a struggle with the British for independence and many of Maharajji's devotees were "freedom fighters" in the cause of Indian independence from Britain, but there is little or nothing in the teaching of Maharajji that supports war and conflict as things to be pursued, let alone won. The supreme consciousness is love, light and bliss. That is what is to be experienced around Maharajji.

The great Baba Jesus predicted that "the meek shall inherit the earth." How right he was, when he said that 2,000 years ago. It may not seem like that yet, but it is true. The people that are alive now are so much more placid than the beings of old. Most of Earth's seven billion people think that it's completely unacceptable to kill another person. Reports in media might make these events seem prevalent, but they are not. These sorts of murders and serial killings are actually much less than, say, 500 years ago. There is a microscope that has been put on human behavior. It is possible to see so much more now.

The thugs and killers are the ones to be shunned, marginalized, and rehabilitated. They are also the most in need of correction. War is an extension of that. It is a completely stupid thing to do. Buddhist have the right idea about this. In Thailand, A young Buddhist monk was passing on a road when a gang of political protestors mindlessly beat him and kicked him. He fell to the ground and passively endured the beating. People running local shops and passersby defended the young monk against the attackers and pulled him away. The monk straightened himself, smoothed his clothes, brushed off the dust, and silently proceeded on his way.

राम राम राम राम राम राम राम राम राम राम राम राम

For the Next Generations

Our Jivatma souls of the future (on the physical-plane timeline) will take birth in an utterly transformed world. The old world with its wrong assumptions and useless fantasies is burning itself out. In this burning, this tapasya, everything negative is rising to the top and is exposed. Do not be afraid of the fire for it is cooking the seeds of the ridiculous human fantasies of greed, hatred, conflict, deception, untruths, psychological control, repression, slavery, male domination, corruption, murder, ego, drug addictions, animal tendencies, and more.

It is an absolutely wonderful marvelous magical world that the human mind has created for the next generations. The kids live in a technological world that formerly would have been called "futurist." We now fly all around the planet. We all read news and eat food and buy goods from all around the planet. We now all know we are even on a planet. These things are universally known all around the world. And our Jivatma is being discovered inside all of us: just as the wonderland of this planet exists on the outer, so too we are all connected to the same inner wonderland. Welcome to a new world of the future. In "Imagine" John Lennon sang, "Imagine no religion." Welcome to a new spirituality. This new spirituality is being discovered within each of us.

Among his many profound statements, Gandhiji said, "The world has enough for everyone's Need, but not enough for everyone's Greed." This is a major realization that must come to all the people of the earth. Surely we will now begin to understand these immortal words.

If you are one of the old ones, the old dinosaurs of this current era, your current body will soon be gone, but when your Jivatma comes back and you have a young body, you will exist in this new wonderland on the physical plane. The kids are inheriting a physical and spiritual world such as has never been known to exist on Earth before. Consciousness has been preparing and building toward this new world for many millennia. Now is the time. Isn't it? Sure. Deep inside you know that is true. Do not look to any sort of media to guide the way. Do not believe in lies. Look into your heart where your Jivatma soul consciousness resides and look to the others who share this understanding with you. Just go there yourself..., with Maharajji.

As Maharajji said, "*Sub thik ho jaega.*" It will be all right. And it is. Enjoy.

राम राम राम राम राम राम राम राम राम राम राम राम

Pushpanjali to Maharajji

To some you say time and again, "Jao, jao...[Go, go...]."
To another, "Jao! [Go Straightaway!]"

Some people you send for, and some
you tell again and again to sit and stay.

To some you tell what observances to follow, to some you teach love,
and in some hearts you light the flame of knowledge.

You send some into yoga nidra [samadhi] for a long time,
and you keep some awake for months, day and night.

You quickly remove the suffering of some,
and in some hearts you increase the pangs of love.

You tell some about their past and some about the present.
For some you foretell a bright future.

Again and again you hail the devotees for their good deeds,
many times extolling their virtues to all.

You increase the riches of some and relieve the anguish of others;
while some find the celestial wealth of contentment.

Some have darshan of their chosen deity at your door;
some have your monkey form established in their hearts.

Once you hold someone's hand, you don't leave them.
Into some ears you pour the nectar-like sacred word.

To the repeated calls of some, you pay no attention,
but to some you give darshan even without being asked.

When some offer a variety of dishes, you are not inclined to take.
But at another's place you take coarse food with relish.

Your mysterious love and affection pours down like heavy rainfall;
the same [love and affection] overflows as tears in the eyes of
devotees.

Some take a sip of your love and weep silently,
and others, overflowing with emotion, cry aloud.

Having come close to you, a learned person may not recognize
you,
but others would say you permeate each and everyone.

Some remain speechless, tasting the nectar of your love,
while some continue singing your praises without satiation.

Some become kings by your grace, and others run after you,
forgetting this world.

Some kings who come to your doorstep cannot have your
darshan,
but some poor souls have your darshan without any effort.

Baba, none can comprehend your Lila;
only those chosen by you can understand.

You console some and relieve the pain of others.

Looking about for the devout ones, you let them drink the nectar of your love.

You save some who are drowning in the ocean of mundane existence,
and you let many float in a flood of your tenderness.

Some you uplift, giving the support of your love
and others you bury in a pile of affection.

Some who are very dear sit in your lap,
whereas some catch a glimpse of you only with great difficulty.

Some get frustrated trying again and again to draw your attention,
but you appear as if you are not at all interested.

Some you awaken, breaking open the doors of their hearts,
and you place in their hands what lay buried inside.

Some you shake up, removing the barriers of the heart,
and you answer the questions that lie unasked in the mind.

"If you have held the hand of a strong one, there is no need of fear."
By saying so you dissipate all fright.

Glory to your abode of Compassion. Your name describes your nature and form.
Who can fathom your endless glory?

Living beings like me, lacking understanding, do not know your beginning or end.
We can only offer flowers of reverence at your feet.

(Part 2)

In utter frustration I write this, begging your grace.
I offer fresh flowers of reverence everyday.

May I sing in praise of you and have devotees as my friends,
and may I take a dip in the river of your love every day.

May I go on getting your prasad and my worldly suffering be
destroyed.
May I go on drinking the water offered at your feet and my heart
be filled with celestial bliss.

I do not desire wealth, fame, or earthly love,
but that I come to your doorstep for your darshan again and
again.

May my tongue take God's name and my mind remain free of
desires,
and may the radiance emanating from the nails of your feet
enlighten my heart.

May my faith and devotion be the cradle in which your image
enjoys swinging,
and may my thoughts be devoted to pushing it all my life.

May I have no feeling for praise or blame
and may I regard this whole world with equal vision.

I have come to your doorstep. Please take my boat across the
ocean of worldly existence.
May I set my hopes only on you and forget about this world.[122]

राम राम राम राम राम राम राम राम राम राम राम राम

About This Book

Maharajji is the ultimate teacher for His devotees. We have learned so much during our years with Maharajji. We trust what Maharajji has shown us much more than what we could possibly have learned from a hundred courses of study in universities. Again and again Maharajji has shown and demonstrated many things to us, as He has with so many other devotees. These have created in us other questions and wonderings. Maharajji has consistently led us to the answers. Yes, this has also been true for all the truly amazing Guru Brothers and Guru Sisters. Each has his or her own path, and Maharajji is the ultimate teacher.

I always took these as my own personal gifts from Maharajji. I never realized that He would some time in my later years, cause me to write these into a book about what I have learned. It never occurred to me to do this until I reached a specific moment when several factors lined up – I happened to be in Chiang Mai Thailand fasting, cleansing, and detoxing at a lovely jungly rural place. I'd arrived from India in a Bhakti state after having the darshan of Mataji and sharing heart-opening time with Maharajji's satsang.

While in the Thailand retreat, I had exchanged emails about Maharajji with a man who runs a spiritual web site. At one point, he asked if I might write something about Maharajji for the site's blog, and I began writing something. After two days, I realized that I was full of information and perspective on Maharajji and a lot of things that Maharajji had guided me to come to understand.

Since I was staying at this retreat in Thailand for several months, I just kept writing and pouring my love of Maharajji, and my amazement with Maharajji's works, into this project. In writing this I have sometimes felt like I've been a toothpaste tube that has been filled up for 30 years and now all this is being squeezed out of me into a text form.

It was necessary to use the "I" word for some stories and perspectives. That couldn't be avoided. Yet none of this book is about me. I am nothing. Maharajji is everything.

Be Love.

राम राम राम राम राम राम राम राम राम राम राम राम

Dedications

This book is dedicated to most beloved Sri Siddhi Ma, the goddess Durga in form on Earth.

To my late wife Radha Rani Rose, a true bhakti, a lover of Lord Krishna, and a magical mataji.

If I were to specifically dedicate this book to anyone (any Westerner) it would be Shivaya Baba. Over the course of some twenty-five years, Shivaya was much more of a Guru to me than anyone. He was my guide to India on my first trip and grounded me in Vrindavan in such a beautiful way that I always remembered him during the many subsequent trips and months living at Maharajji's ashram on Parikrama Marg. To this day, I still treasure the many hours of one-on-one time we shared over many years in Taos, and India, and Marin. While Shivaya lived in Taos, we spent many hours in "dharma talks" and I gained immeasurably from these. Shivaya was a true Badmash (rascal) who spent years as a sadhu in India, had met so many of the saints and sages of India, and most importantly had taken the darshan of Maharajji. Although he arrived with the name Avram and Maharajji called him Gandhiji, the very appropriate name Shivaya stuck. Shivaya's wit and wisdom, as well has his legendary fierceness are many of my fondest satsang memories. I am not sure that Shivaya would agree with everything I have written in this book, although he taught me or guided me on the path of learning about several things herein. Shivaya unabashedly told me when I was right and when I was wrong. I wish he were here with us still, so that he could give some some guidance about some things in this book, much like we'd shared a lot during the early years that I was making Maharajji's global Web site. Shivaya taught me to fearlessly take my place in the cast of characters in the theater of Maharajji's Lilas. After several weeks of quality time in Vrindavan together in 2008, I'm sorry to say, we had too few hours together. The last time I saw Shivaya was at the last birthday party for Dasaratha in Santa Fe in August 2012. It was the last time I saw Das and Geoffrey Gordon, too. These are three beloveds that are much missed. The last time I spoke on the phone with Shivaya, he said "I've always enjoyed hanging out with you. Catch you next time." Yeah. In 2013, I was in Thailand when Ravi Das told me that Shivaya Baba had left his body. *Ram nam satya hai.* His beloved wife Uma cared for him. Shivaya said, "We believe in miracles and we believe in reincarnation," so I am certain that we have met and will meet again in other lives. Shivaya was one of the most amazing close friends I've ever had. I love him a lot and I always felt his love for me, too.

And dedicated to Sadhu Ma. She was my beloved Gurusister/brother. She was many things to many people and had an extraordinary life. She welcomed me into Maharajji's satsang from the very beginning. She was one of the best songwriters I ever met, preferred devotion to Maharajji, did not seek commercial success, and ultimately took all her songs with her when she left her body.

And dedicated to Lillian North. During the later years of her life Lillian lived in Taos. Lillian was a wonderful lady who was our "elder" here for years. Much of Lillian's day was spent sitting at her kitchen table with visiting devotees. Lillian spent almost every moment focused on the dharma. She often demanded we engage in "dharma talks." A very fierce and loving lady who served Maharajji and the dharma in many ways, including being partially responsible for instigating the book "Be Here Now" by Ram Dass.

Dedicated to Guru brothers and Guru sisters on Maharajji's trail: Americans: Hari Das, Krishna, Gangaram, Hanuman Das, Dwarka, Gauri, Lakshmi, Ram Rani, Daya, Gauri Dassi, Satrupa, Mohan Baba, Sita Sharan, Kabir Das, Ram Charan Bihari Lal, Uma & Vishwarnath, Rameshwardas, Raghu, Parvati, Ira. Indians: Gurudat Sharma, Dharma Narayan Sharma, Rabboo Joshi, Baba C. S. Sharma, Bobby Bhatele, Usha Bahadur, Dr. (Mrs) Saroj Pandey, Bhoskar, Vinod, Urvashi Bhatia.   Globals: Ram Dass, Krishna Das, Jai Uttal.

Special Thanks to my beloved Lee Boothby - Lila's encouragement and advice (via Skype between Thailand and Taos), and her extra effort in helping me edit and correct the first versions of the manuscript helped make this book possible.

Special Thanks to Patrick J. Finn for helping me complete the final aspects of making this book available in printed book and ebook forms.

In remembrance of: Dasaratha Marcus, Geoffrey Gordon, Shyam Das, Bo Lazoff, and Swami Ram Tiertha.

राम राम राम राम राम राम राम राम राम राम राम राम

"You should do your work, be friendly to everyone, and never quarrel with anyone. People who are jealous of you will oppose you in various ways but do not take it to heart. Do your work like a great hero and all will be well for you."
Maharajji

राम राम राम राम राम राम राम राम राम राम राम राम
राम राम राम राम राम राम राम राम राम राम राम राम
राम राम राम राम राम राम राम राम राम राम राम राम
राम राम राम राम राम राम राम राम राम राम राम राम
राम राम राम राम राम राम राम राम राम राम राम राम

Endnotes

The Endnotes may prove a bit helpful as a sort of "cookbook" for some further study of Maharajji Neem Karoli Baba,, Hindu Practice, Theology, Consciousness, and the Dharma.

राम राम राम राम राम राम राम राम राम राम राम राम

[1] More information about Maharajji's Vrindavan Ashram: http://maharajji.com/Vrindavan/vrindavan-ashram.html.

[2] In Hinduism, an avatar /ˈævətɑr/ (Hindustani: [əʊˈtaːr], from Sanskrit अवतार avatāra "descent") is a deliberate descent of a deity to Earth,

or a descent of the Supreme Being (e.g., Vishnu for Vaishnavites), and is mostly translated into English as "incarnation," but more accurately as "appearance" or "manifestation." - excerpt from Wikipedia under Creative Commons license. More about avatar here: http://en.wikipedia.org/wiki/Avatar.

[3] A kōan is a story, dialogue, question, or statement, which is used in Zen-practice to provoke the "great doubt," and test a student's progress in Zen practice. Source: Wikipedia under Creative Commons license. More about Koan here: http://en.wikipedia.org/wiki/Kōan.

[4] More information about Akbarpur, the birthplace of Maharajji: http://maharajji.com/Akbarpur/akbarpur-maharajjis-birthplace.html.

[5] Excerpt from "Prem Avatar" by Mukunda. This book is published in Hindi. Some of this book is published in small booklets in Hindi and English under title "Prem Avatar." Text herein is excerpted from unpublished English manuscripts. Online excerpts at: http://maharajji.com/Premavatar/prem-avatar.html.

[6] From Wikipedia under Creative Commons License. More about Siddhis here: https://en.wikipedia.org/wiki/Siddhis.

[7] Written by Jai Ram, from http://maharajji.com/About-Maharajji/what-about-maharajjis-names.html.

[8] The term " sādhanā" means spiritual exertion towards an intended goal. A person undertaking such a practice is known as a sādhu or a sādhaka. The goal of sādhanā is to attain some level of spiritual realization, which can be either enlightenment, pure love of God (prema), liberation (moksha) from the cycle of birth and death (saṃsāra), or a particular goal such as the blessings of a deity as in the Bhakti traditions.

Sādhanā can involve meditation, chanting of mantra (sometimes with the help of a japa mala), puja to a deity, yajna, and in very rare cases mortification of the flesh or tantric practices such as performing one's particular sādhanā within a cremation ground.

from Wikipedia under Creative Commons License. More about Sadhana here: http://en.wikipedia.org/wiki/Sadhana.

[9] Excerpt from "By His Grace: A Devotee's Story" by Sudhir 'Dada' Mukerjee; Publisher: Hanuman Foundation; ISBN-10: 0962887870; ISBN-13: 978-0962887871.

[10] Reference to Bhagavad Gita. Recommended Reading: For further study, an excellent version is "The Bhagavad Gita" translated by Eknath Easwaran, Publisher: Knopf Doubleday, ISBN-13: 9780375705557.

[11] Excerpt from "I and My Father are One" by Rabboo Joshi. Publisher: Rabindra Kumar Joshi, New Delhi India; ISBN: 978-81-908843-0-3.

[12] Excerpts From: Bart D. Ehrman. "How Jesus Became God." Publisher: Harper One, ISBN-10: 0061778184, ISBN-13: 978-0061778186.

[13] Aarti is part of puja. Aarti is performed during almost all Hindu ceremonies and occasions. It involves the circulating of an 'Aarti plate' or 'Aarti lamp' around a person or deity and is generally accompanied by the singing of songs in praise of that deva or person (many versions exist). In doing so, the plate or lamp is supposed to acquire the power of the deity. The priest circulates the plate or lamp to all those present. They cup their down-turned hands over the flame and then raise their palms to their forehead – the purificatory blessing, passed from the deva's image to the flame, has now been passed to the devotee. For more about aarti, consult: http://en.wikipedia.org/wiki/Aarti.

[14] About Nishkam Karma: The opposite of Sakam Karma (Attached Involvement) or actions done with results in mind, Nishkam Karma has been variously explained as 'Duty for duty's sake' and as 'Detached Involvement', which is neither negative attitude or indifference..., from Wikipedia. For more about Nishkam Karma, consult: http://en.wikipedia.org/wiki/Nishkam_Karma.

[15] Excerpt from "The Divine Reality of Sri Baba Neeb Karori Ji Maharaj (A Translation of Alokik Yathartha)" by Rajida. Publisher: Sri Kainchi Hanuman Mandir & Ashram; ISBN-10: 819031050X, ISBN-13: 978-8190310505.

[16] "lilas and kathas" - is unclear because the transcriber could not discern what was said on the recording and used these words as an approximation.

[17] Excerpt from "Prem Avatar" by Mukunda. This book is published in Hindi. Some of this book is published in small booklets in Hindi and English under title "Prem Avatar." Text herein is excerpted from unpublished English manuscripts. Online excerpts at: http://maharajji.com/Premavatar/prem-avatar.html.

[18] The schools of Vedānta seek to answer questions about the relation between atman and Brahman, and the relation between Brahman and the world.

The schools of Vedanta are named after the relation they see between atman and Brahman: According to Advaita Vedanta, there is no difference. According to Dvaita the jīvātman is totally different from Brahman. Even though he is similar to brahman, he is not identical. According to Vishishtadvaita, the jīvātman is a part of Brahman, and hence is similar, but not identical.

Sivananda gives the following explanation: Madhva said: "Man is the servant of God," and established his Dvaita philosophy. Ramanuja said: "Man is a ray or spark of God," and established his Visishtadvaita philosophy. Sankara said: "Man is identical with Brahman or the Eternal Soul," and established his Kevala Advaita philosophy.

Excerpt from Wikipedia under Creative Commons License. More about Vedānta here: https://en.wikipedia.org/wiki/Vedanta.

[19] Excerpt from Wikipedia under Creative Commons License. More about Nirvana here: http://en.wikipedia.org/wiki/Nirvana.

[20] Dea has five aspects: existence, consciousness, bliss, name and form (*sat-chit-ananda-nama-rupa*). *Sat, chit, ananda* are the real aspects (*satya amsas*), *nama and rupa* are the unreal aspects (*mithya amsas*). The three real aspects can be likened to gold, the true substance or reality (*vastu*), while the latter two can be likened to ornaments made from gold. Whereas gold is permanent and unchanging, its names and forms, the ornaments, are transient and subject to change.

The difference between the one who is ignorant, the *ajnani*, and the one who knows, the *jnani*, is that in the experience of the *ajnani*, the "I" is limited to the measure of the body, that is, to the *nama* and *rupa*, the name and form of the body, whereas in the experience of the *jnani*, the "I" shines as the limitless Dea, without whom the body cannot exist. The *ajnani* thinks that the body alone is "I," like the one who thinks that the ornament alone is gold, whereas the *jnani* experiences that the body is also "I," like one who understands that the ornament is also gold. From: http:// eternalfeminine.wikispaces.com/The+Five+Aspects+of+Dea.

[21] As told to Jai Ram, from http://maharajji.com/Experiences-With-Maharajji/from-gurudat-sharma.html.

[22] Excerpt from "Be Love Now: The Path of the Heart" by Ram Dass and Rameshwar Das, Publisher: HarperCollins; ASIN: B003VIWO3Y.

[23] Max Karl Ernst Ludwig Planck was a German theoretical physicist who originated quantum theory, which won him the Nobel Prize in Physics in 1918. Planck made many contributions to theoretical physics, but his fame rests primarily on his role as originator of the quantum theory. This theory revolutionized human understanding of atomic and subatomic processes, just as Albert Einstein's theory of relativity revolutionized the understanding of space and time. Together they constitute the fundamental theories of 20th-century physics. — http://www.goodreads.com/author/show/107032. Max_Planck and http://en.wikipedia.org/wiki/Max_Planck.

[24] Excerpt from: Dr. Larry Dossey, Huffington Post, http:// www.huffingtonpost.com/dr-larry-dossey/is-consciousness-the-cent_b_645069.html.

[25] More information about Baba Ram Dass can be found at ramdass.org.

26 The Vedas (Sanskrit véda वेद, "knowledge") are a large body of texts originating in ancient India. Composed in Vedic Sanskrit, the texts constitute the oldest layer of Sanskrit literature and the oldest scriptures of Hinduism. The Vedas are apauruṣeya ("not of human agency"). They are supposed to have been directly revealed, and thus are called śruti ("what is heard"), distinguishing them from other religious texts, which are called smṛti ("what is remembered"). In Hindu tradition, the creation of Vedas is credited to Brahma. - More about the Vedas here: http://en.wikipedia.org/wiki/Vedas.

27 Reference to "Seth Speaks," as channeled by Jane Roberts.

28 Reference to: "The Seth Material" by Jane Roberts.

29 Reference to: "Autobiography of a Yogi" by ParamahansaYogananda.

30 Kriya Yoga, as taught by Lahiri Mahasaya, is traditionally exclusively learned via the Guru-disciple relationship and the initiation consists of a secret ceremony. He recounted that after his initiation into Kriya Yoga, "Babaji instructed me in the ancient rigid rules which govern the transmission of the yogic art from Guru to disciple."

As Yogananda describes Kriya Yoga, "The Kriya Yogi mentally directs his life energy to revolve, upward and downward, around the six spinal centers (medullary, cervical, dorsal, lumbar, sacral, and coccygeal plexuses) which correspond to the twelve astral signs of the zodiac, the symbolic Cosmic Man. One half-minute of revolution of energy around the sensitive spinal cord of man effects subtle progress in his evolution; that half-minute of Kriya equals one year of natural spiritual unfoldment."

In Kriya Quotes from Swami Satyananda, it is written, "Kriya sadhana may be thought of as the sadhana of the "practice of being in Atman."

Source: Wikipedia under Creative Commons license. More about Kriya Yoga here: http://en.wikipedia.org/wiki/Kriya_Yoga.

31 Sorry. The author can neither find nor remember who said this, but it's relevant, as well a rather beautiful.

32 A chillum is a cone shaped clay pipe in which a hashish and tobacco blend is smoked.

33 Excerpt from http://www.druglibrary.org/schaffer/hemp/history/first12000/1.htm.

[34] "Lama Foundation is a spiritual community, educational facility, and retreat center adjacent to the Carson National Forest about 30 miles south of Colorado near the town of Taos, New Mexico. Designed as a community that embraces all spiritual traditions, it has strong ties to Taos Pueblo, the Hanuman Temple in Taos, NM, Sufi Ruhaniat International, Dervish Healing Order, The Church of Conscious Harmony, St. Benedict's Monastery in Snowmass, CO, and dozens of other communities, spiritual teachers, and thousands of pilgrims from nearly all religious heritages who call Lama their home." - from Lama Foundation Web site, http://www.lamafoundation.org/.

[35] Excerpt from "By His Grace: A Devotee's Story" by Sudhir 'Dada' Mukerjee; Publisher: Hanuman Foundation; ISBN-10: 0962887870; ISBN-13: 978-0962887871.

[36] From Lee Boothby, author of "Mind Power" and a most helpful sevak in preparing this book for publication.

[37] Excerpt from "By His Grace: A Devotee's Story" by Sudhir 'Dada' Mukerjee; Publisher: Hanuman Foundation; ISBN-10: 0962887870; ISBN-13: 978-0962887871.

[38] Excerpt from Wikipedia under Creative Commons License. More about Advaita here: https://en.wikipedia.org/wiki/Advaita_Vedanta.

[39] from Mukunda's Book "Prem Avatar," http://maharajji.com/Premavatar/maharajji-cures-kehar-singhji.html.

[40] Laozi (also spelled Lao-Tzu; Lao-tze) was a philosopher and poet of ancient China. He is best known as the reputed author of the Tao Te Ching and the founder of philosophical Taoism, but he is also revered as a deity in religious Taoism and traditional Chinese religions. From Wikipedia under Creative Commons License. More about Lao Tzu here: http://en.wikipedia.org/wiki/Lao_Tsu.

[41] More information about HWL Poonja (Papaji): http://avadhuta.com/.

[42] http://www.nytimes.com/2014/02/16/opinion/sunday/is-the-universe-a-simulation.html?_r=0.

[43] Refers to a story in "Miracle of Love: Stories About Neem Karoli Baba" by Ram Dass, First Publisher: Plume; ISBN-10: 0525482504; ISBN-13: 978-0525482505, Second Publisher: Hanuman Foundation; ISBN-10: 1887474005; ISBN-13: 978-1887474009, Third Publisher: Penguin Books; ISBN-10: 0140193413; ISBN-13: 978-0140193411.

[44] As my mentor, Gurudat Sharma is one of the five people whose feet I touch in India.

[45] Excerpt from: http://www.iloveindia.com/indian-traditions/touching-feet.html.

[46] Excerpt from "By His Grace: A Devotee's Story" by Sudhir 'Dada' Mukerjee; Publisher: Hanuman Foundation; ISBN-10: 0962887870; ISBN-13: 978-0962887871. Taken from: http://maharajji.com/By-His-Grace/kainchi.html.

[47] Excerpt from http://maharajji.com/Experiences-With-Maharajji/from-gurudat-sharma.html.

[48] Excerpt from "It's Here Now (Are You?)" by Bhagavan Das, Publisher: Harmony; ISBN-10: 076790009X; ISBN-13: 978-0767900096.

[49] Kirtan or kirtana (In Hindi: कीर्तन) - Kirtan practice involves chanting hymns or mantras to the accompaniment of instruments such as the harmonium, tablas, the two-headed mrdanga or pakhawaj drum and hand cymbals (karatalas). It is a major practice in Vaisnava devotionalism, Sikhism, the Sant traditions and some forms of Buddhism, as well as other religious groups. It is often suggested as the form of religious activity best suited to the present age. - except from Wikipedia under Creative Commons License. More about kirtan here: http://en.wikipedia.org/wiki/Kirtan.

[50] From Gurudat Sharma - http://maharajji.com/Experiences-With-Maharajji/from-gurudat-sharma.html.

[51] Reference to: "Jesus Lived in India: His Unknown Life Before and After the Crucifixion" by Holger Kersten. Publisher: Penguin, ISBN-10: 0143028294, ISBN-13: 978-0143028291. Publisher: Element Books, ISBN-10: 0906540909, ISBN-13: 978-0906540909.

[52] More information about Taos Hanuman Temple at Neem Karoli Baba Ashram, New Mexico can be found at: http://www.nkbashram.org/.

[53] More information about Kashi Ashram, Florida can be found at: http://www.kashi.org/.

[54] Excerpt from "The Sacred Wanderer" by Ravi Das, Publisher: Sacred Wanderer Productions; Page Numbers Source ISBN: 0615344887, ASIN: B003XKNWFO.

[55] More information about Masaru Emoto here: http://www.masaru-emoto.net/english/.

[56] Excerpt from "The Near and the Dear" by Dada Mukurjee, Publisher: Hanuman Foundation; ISBN-10: 1887474021; ISBN-13: 978-1887474023.

[57] Excerpt from Wikipedia under Creative Commons License. More about seva here: http://en.wikipedia.org/wiki/Selfless_service.

[58] Puri is an unleavened deep-fried Indian bread, commonly consumed on the Indian subcontinent. It is eaten for breakfast or as a snack or light meal. It is usually served with a curry or bhaji, as in Puri bhaji. Puri is most commonly served at breakfast. It is also served at special or ceremonial functions as part of ceremonial rituals along with other vegetarian food offered in prayer as prasadam. The name puri derives from the Sanskrit word पूरिका (pūrikā), from पुर (pura) "filled." [58] from Wikipedia under Creative Commons License. More about Puri here: http://en.wikipedia.org/wiki/Puri_(food).

[59] From Gurudat Sharma - http://maharajji.com/Experiences-With-Maharajji/from-gurudat-sharma.html.

[60] Excerpt from Wikipedia under Creative Commons License. More about tapasya here: http://en.wikipedia.org/wiki/Tapasya.

[61] Khir is a delicious sweet made from rice, milk and spices, usually served warm.

[62] Braj (Hindi/Braj Bhasha: ब्रज) (also known as Brij or Brajbhoomi) is a region mainly in Uttar Pradesh of India, around Mathura-Vrindavan. Braj, though never a clearly defined political region in India, is very well demarcated culturally. It is considered to be the land of Krishna and is derived from the Sanskrit word vraja. The main cities in the region are Mathura, Bharatpur, Agra, Hathras, Dholpur, Aligarh, Etawah, Mainpuri, Etah, Kasganj and Firozabad. More about Braj here: http://en.wikipedia.org/wiki/Braj.

[63] Japa (Sanskrit: जप) is a spiritual discipline involving the meditative repetition of a mantra or name of a divine power. The practice can also involve the repetitive writing of names of God, as Maharajji wrote Rams.

[64] Excerpt from "It's Here Now (Are You?)" by Bhagavan Das, Publisher: Harmony; ISBN-10: 076790009X; ISBN-13: 978-0767900096.

[65] From http://maharajji.com/Experiences-With-Maharajji/from-gurudat-sharma.html.

[66] "quote or bhagvad" - is unclear because the transcriber could not discern what was said on the recording and used these words as an approximation.

[67] Excerpt from "Prem Avatar" by Mukunda. This book is published in Hindi. Some of this book is published in small booklets in Hindi and English under title "Prem Avatar." Text herein is excerpted from unpublished English manuscripts. Online excerpts at: http://maharajji.com/Premavatar/prem-avatar.html.

[68] Excerpt from "Prem Avatar" by Mukunda. This book is published in Hindi. Some of this book is published in small booklets in Hindi and English under title "Prem Avatar." Text herein is excerpted from unpublished English manuscripts. Online excerpts at: http://maharajji.com/Premavatar/prem-avatar.html.

[69] Maharajji's kutir in Kainchi was jokingly called "Maharajji's Office" by the young Western devotees. Due to this, there is a semi-private meditation room at Maharajji's Taos Ashram in USA that is referred to as "Maharajji's Office" by devotees.

[70] Excerpt from "It's Here Now (Are You?)" by Bhagavan Das, Publisher: Harmony; ISBN-10: 076790009X; ISBN-13: 978-0767900096.

[71] Excerpt from "I and My Father are One" by Rabboo Joshi. Publisher: Rabindra Kumar Joshi, New Delhi India; ISBN: 978-81-908843-0-3.

[72] "And to the angel of the church in Philadelphia write; These things saith he that is holy, he that is true, he that hath the key of David, he that openeth, and no man shutteth; and shutteth, and no man openeth." - The Revelation of St, John the Divine. 3:7.

[73] I salute the dust of the feet of the Guru, I remember the pure name of the Guru, I adore the beautiful form of the Guru, I sing the glorious evil-destroying praises of the Guru. – Sri Guru Stotra. http://maharajji.com/Sri-Guru-Stotra/sri-guru-stotra-english.html.

[74] Excerpt from "Barefoot in the Heart: Remembering Neem Karoli Baba" edited by Keshav Das. Publisher: Sensitive Skin Books, ISBN-978-0-9839271-3-6.

[75] Excerpt from "Miracle of Love: Stories About Neem Karoli Baba" by Ram Dass, First Publisher: Plume; ISBN-10: 0525482504; ISBN-13: 978-0525482505, Second Publisher: Hanuman Foundation; ISBN-10: 1887474005; ISBN-13: 978-1887474009, Third Publisher: Penguin Books; ISBN-10: 0140193413; ISBN-13: 978-0140193411.

[76] "Mas" is a general term referring to groups of older devotee ladies, often widows. Ma is derived from Mataji, or Mother. This term is very much in use today.

[77] Buti is sacred flame made with cotton and ghee held in an aarti lamp.

[78] Written by Jai Ram, from http://maharajji.com/Experiences-With-Maharajji/from-gurudat-sharma.html.

[79] More information about Practice at Maharajji's temples can be found here: http://maharajji.com/Table/Practice/.

[80] For complete versions in English, Hindi and transliteration of Jaya Jagadish Hare, go to: maharajji.com/Practice/Jaya-Jagadisha-Hare/.

[81] For complete versions in English, Hindi, transliteration and word by word Hindi/English translation of Hanuman Chalisa at: http://maharajji.com/Practice/Hanuman-Chalisa/.

[82] For complete versions in English, Hindi and transliteration of Hanuman Astoka at: http://maharajji.com/Practice/Hanuman-Astaka/.

[83] For complete versions in English, Hindi and transliteration of Vinaya Chalisa at: http://maharajji.com/Practice/Vinaya-Chalisa/.

[84] For complete versions in English, Hindi and transliteration of Sri Guru Stotra at: http://maharajji.com/Practice/Sri-Guru-Stotra/.

[85] Kali Yuga (Devanāgarī: कलियुग [kəli jugə], lit. "age of [the demon] Kali," or "age of vice") is the last of the four stages the world goes through as part of the cycle of yugas described in the Indian scriptures. The other ages are Satya Yuga, Treta Yuga and Dvapara Yuga.

Kali Yuga is associated with the apocalyptic demon Kali, not to be confused with the goddess Kālī. The "Kali" of Kali Yuga means "strife," "discord," "quarrel" or "contention."

from Wikipedia under Creative Commons License. More about Kali Yuga here: http://en.wikipedia.org/wiki/Kali_Yuga.

[86] Learn More at: http://www.krishnadas.com/chanting.cfm.

[87] Learn More at: http://jaiuttal.com/kirtan/.

[88] Sri Prabhudayal Sharma R/O Mathura -Agra.

[89] Pukka (Hindi पक्का, Urdu پکّا pakkā) is a word of Hindi and Urdu origin, literally meaning "cooked, ripe" and figuratively "fully formed," "solid," "permanent," "for real" or "sure." In UK slang, it can mean "genuine" or simply "very good." - from Wikipedia under Creative Commons License.

[90] Excerpt from Wikipedia under Creative Commons License. For more about Ishta Devata, visit: http://en.wikipedia.org/wiki/Ishta_Devata.

[91] Source: from Wikipedia under Creative Commons License. From Keshavadas, SadGuru Sant (1988). "Aranya Kanda." Ramayana at a Glance. Motilal Banarsidass. p. 124. ISBN 978-81-208-0545-3.

[92] Kainchi means "scissors" in Hindi, so named because Maharajji's ashram there is in a very narrow valley with very steep sides.

[93] Excerpt from "The Divine Reality of Sri Baba Neeb Karori Ji Maharaj (A Translation of Alokik Yathartha)" by Rajida. Publisher: Sri Kainchi Hanuman Mandir & Ashram; ISBN-10: 819031050X, ISBN-13: 978-8190310505.

[94] Excerpt from "The Essential Alan Watts."

[95] Yātrā (Sanskrit: यात्रा, 'journey', 'procession'), in Hinduism and other Indian religions, generally means pilgrimage to holy places such as confluences of sacred rivers, places associated with Hindu epics such as the Mahabharata and Ramayana, and other sacred pilgrimage sites. Source: Wikipedia, used under Creative Commons License. More about yatra here: http://en.wikipedia.org/wiki/Yatra.

[96] In 1940, French statesman Baron DePonnat stated "Roman Catholicism was born in blood, has wallowed in blood, and has quenched its thirst in blood, and it is in letters of blood that its true history is written." Indeed, the history of papal Rome has been one of brutal torture, slaughter, and mass murder. During the six centuries of papal Inquisition that began in the 13th century, up to 50 million people were killed. - excerpt from http://rekindlingthereformation.com/RTR-Articles-Papal-Rome-Timeline.html.

[97] Excerpt from Wikipedia under Creative Commons License. From http://en.wikipedia.org/wiki/Ahimsa.

[98] Excerpt from Wikipedia under Creative Commons License. From http://en.wikipedia.org/wiki/Emperor_Ashoka.

[99] Excerpt from "Prem Avatar" by Mukunda. This book is published in Hindi. Some of this book is published in small booklets in Hindi and English under title "Prem Avatar." Text herein is excerpted from unpublished English manuscripts. Online excerpts at: http://maharajji.com/Premavatar/prem-avatar.html.

[100] To read the full story: http://maharajji.com/Near-and-the-Dear/story-of-the-leaf-plates.html.

[101] Excerpt from "The Divine Reality of Sri Baba Neeb Karori Ji Maharaj (A Translation of Alokik Yathartha)" by Rajida. Publisher: Sri Kainchi Hanuman Mandir & Ashram; ISBN-10: 819031050X, ISBN-13: 978-8190310505.

[102] More information about Maharajji's Kainchi Ashram: http://maharajji.com/Kainchi/kainchi-ashram.html.

[103] Written by Jai Ram, from http://maharajji.com/Experiences-With-Maharajji/from-usha-bahadur.html.

[104] More information about Maharajji's Paniki Hanuman Temple: http://maharajji.com/Kanpur/paniki-hanuman-temple-in-kanpur.html.

[105] Vrindavan Parikrama is a spiritual walk undertaken by devotees around Vrindavan town in Uttar Pradesh. It has no particular start or end place. As long as you end at the same place you start, the purpose is served. - Source: Wikipedia under Creative Commons License. More about Parikrama here: http://en.wikipedia.org/wiki/Parikrama

[106] The Chota Char Dham (Devanagari: चार धाम) (literally translated as 'the small four abodes/seats', meaning 'the small circuit of four abodes/seats'), is an important Hindu pilgrimage circuit in the Indian Himalayas. Located in the Garhwal region of the state of Uttarakhand (formerly the northwestern section of Uttar Pradesh), the circuit consists of four sites—Yamunotri (Hindi: यमनोत्री), Gangotri (Hindi: गंगोत्री), Kedarnath (Hindi: केदारनाथ), and Badrinath (Hindi: बद्रीनाथ).[1] Badrinath is also one of the four destinations (with each destination being in different corners of the country) of the longer Char Dham from which the Chota Char Dham likely draws its name. - Source: Wikipedia under Creative Commons License. More about Chota Char Dham here: http://en.wikipedia.org/wiki/Chota_Char_Dham

[107] Information about Maharajji's ashrams and temples: http://maharajji.com/Ashrams-Temples/.

[108] More information about Taos Hanuman Temple at Neem Karoli Baba Ashram, New Mexico can be found at: http://www.nkbashram.org/.

[109] No Eggs/Garlic/Onions in food - EGO: these present a "hurdle" on the path to the effects the ashram is to achieve in you.

[110] A dhuni is (according to the dharmic religions such as Hinduism, Buddhism, Jainism, etc.) a sacred site represented as a cleft in the ground. This cleft is emblematic of the yoni or female vulva and generative organ. A dhuni therefore represents a site of worship dedicated to Shakti.

A dhuni is worshipped by spiritual intention and the kindling of a flame inside it. Suitable materials are offered to the dhuni and consumed by the heat or flame. This represents the eternal process of change and transformation on all levels of existence.

"Like a river, a dhuni is always changing. Each dhuni also has its own personality that is as much subject to moods as a person. The glow of the dhuni is both a receiver and a transmitter, and like a screen on which Rorschach-like images are projected, it delivers a code."

As the yoni is the nexus from which all manifest beings come into this world, the worship of the dhuni represents a sacred nexus for the path of return from the physical to spiritual level. This is an intentional process of inversion or return to our spiritual source. The dhuni is a sacred site and focal point for this form of spiritual exertion or sadhana.

Aside from the offering of sacred fuel to a dhuni, mantras are also offered, as well as the sounds of diverse musical instruments and ecstatic dance and gesture.

Although several cultures retain traditions of fire worship (out of which the zorastrianism is perhaps the most famous), a unique feature of the dhuni tradition is that it is the dhuni, the actual site itself which is considered sacred, not exclusively the fire kindled within it.

Sai Baba of Shirdi is certainly the most influential modern "Supersoul" to tend the Dhuni which he kept lit at that place until October 15, 1918 when he moved on.

Source: Wikipedia under Creative Commons License. More about dhuni here: http://en.wikipedia.org/wiki/Dhuni.

[111] From The Near and the Dear, K.C. Tewari about Maharajji. http://maharajji.com/Near-and-the-Dear/k-c-tewari-chapter.html.

[112] This is an Eckist teaching and is probably loosely derived from Hinduism.

[113] Gallery of Photos of Maharajji: http://maharajji.com/photos-of-maharajji.

[114] A beedi (/ˈbiːdiː/; from Hindi: बीड़ी; also spelled bidi or biri) is a thin, Indian cigarette filled with tobacco flake and wrapped in a tendu or possibly even Piliostigma racemosum leaf tied with a string at one end. - from Wikipedia under Creative Commons License.

[115] Written by Jai Ram, Taos, from http://maharajji.com/Recent-Devotees-Experiences/why-i-dont-smoke-on-maharajjis-porch.html."

[116] Excerpt from "Miracle of Love: Stories About Neem Karoli Baba" by Ram Dass, First Publisher: Plume; ISBN-10: 0525482504; ISBN-13: 978-0525482505, Second Publisher: Hanuman Foundation; ISBN-10: 1887474005; ISBN-13: 978-1887474009, Third Publisher: Penguin Books; ISBN-10: 0140193413; ISBN-13: 978-0140193411.

[117] Excerpt from "Prem Avatar" by Mukunda. This book is published in Hindi. Some of this book is published in small booklets in Hindi and English under title "Prem Avatar." Text herein is excerpted from unpublished English manuscripts. Online excerpts at: http://maharajji.com/Premavatar/prem-avatar.html.

[118] Transcript of Krishna Das [krishnadas.com] speaking in a radio interview with Radha Fournier, Heart of the Islands Satsang [http://www.heartoftheislandssatsang.com] 2012.

[119] Excerpt from "The Divine Reality of Sri Baba Neeb Karori Ji Maharaj (A Translation of Alokik Yathartha)" by Rajida. Publisher: Sri Kainchi Hanuman Mandir & Ashram; ISBN-10: 819031050X, ISBN-13: 978-8190310505.

[120] From http://maharajji.com/Experiences-With-Maharajji/from-usha-bahadur.html.

[121] Reference to "Living with the Himalayan Masters" by Swami Rama; Publisher: Himalayan Institute Press; ASIN: B002RHONU2.

[122] "Pushpanjali to Maharajji}, written by Sri Prabhudayal Sharma R/O Mathura -Agra. From: http://maharajji.com/Practice/Pushpanjali/.

Pushpanjali is an offering of flowers to Indian Gods. In Sanskrit, pushpam means "flower" and anjali means "offering with folded hands." Thus, Pushpanjali means "offering of flowers with folded hands."